HOW TO PREACH

**A Practical Guide
to Better Sermons**

HOW TO PREACH

**A Practical Guide to
Better Sermons**

Steven P. Vitrano

ℝ

REVIEW AND HERALD® PUBLISHING ASSOCIATION
HAGERSTOWN, MD 21740

Copyright © 1991 by
Review and Herald® Publishing Association

The author assumes full responsibility for the accuracy of all facts and quotations as cited in this book.

Unless otherwise noted all scriptural passages are from the Revised Standard Version of the Bible, copyright © 1946, 1952, 1971, by the Division of Christian Education of the National Council of the Churches of Christ in the U.S.A. Used by permission.

This book was
Edited by Richard W. Coffen
Designed by Bill Kirstein
Cover art by Helcio Deslandes
Typeset: 11/12 Garamond Book

PRINTED IN U.S.A.

96 95 94 93 92 91   10 9 8 7 6 5 4 3 2 1

Library of Congress Cataloging in Publication Data

Vitrano, Steven P.
    How to preach: a practical guide to better sermons / Steven P.
Vitrano.
        p.   cm.
    Includes bibliographical references.
    1. Preaching.   I. Title.
BV4211.2.V57   1991
    251—dc20

91-34922
CIP

ISBN 0-8280-0649-0

Contents

Introduction 7

Chapter 1 What Is Preaching? 9

Chapter 2 The Sermon 18

Chapter 3 Preaching Textually 31

Chapter 4 Other Options 42

Chapter 5 Starting, Stopping, and Opening the Windows 55

Chapter 6 Preaching the Sermon 64

Chapter 7 The Preacher 74

Chapter 8 Give It Your Best 87

Bibliography 90

Other Books by Steven P. Vitrano

God's Way of Righting Wrong

An Hour of Good News

So You're Not a Preacher

Introduction

Every Sabbath, in thousands of Seventh-day Adventist churches, laypeople are called upon to preach during the hour of worship. They may also have the responsibility of conducting a prayer meeting during the week or of giving a devotional talk or Bible study upon some other occasion. They are not "preachers." They have not been formally trained as clergymen. They are local lay leaders, most of whom are persons who have been ordained to the office of church elder. Many of them do an acceptable and commendable job, but many also need help. They hardly know where to begin in preparation for the task they face, and they feel self-conscious and insecure in what they are trying to do. It is for them that this book is written.

This work is not intended to be a learned treatise on preaching. It is written in full knowledge of the fact that homiletics in its broader sense involves much more than the "mechanics" of how to construct a sermon. For this reason I had to make some difficult decisions about what to include and what to exclude. I hope that this book will fulfill a need that is somewhat specific to the Seventh-day Adventist Church, and I dedicate it to a special type of preacher. I pray that it will be practical and therefore useful.

CHAPTER

1

What Is Preaching?

You have served as a local church elder for several months. One morning the pastor calls: "I'll be out of the district for several days three weeks from now. Would you be willing to preach the sermon on Sabbath morning?"

"Me? Preach the sermon? Are you serious? I can't preach!"

"Of course you can. Surely you've given a talk or a speech some time or other."

"But that's not *preaching*."

You're right! Preaching a sermon is not the same as giving a talk or delivering a speech. But why not? What's so special about preaching? That question has been asked—and answered—again and again. New books on the subject appear in print every year. But when you are asked to fill the role of preacher, questions as to the nature and means of preaching become critically relevant to *you*. The answers do not have to be final, but they certainly had better be practical!

This manual on preaching is designed to help you find just those kinds of answers—practical answers to questions that people such as you might have about preaching. It begins by giving some consideration to the "what" of preaching, because for practical as well as theological reasons your attitude toward preaching is really more important than how you preach. The "what" should cause one to take more seriously and give better attention to the "how." In Paul's first letter to the Thessalonians he makes a significant statement as to what preaching is all about: "For you remember our labor and toil, brethren; we worked night and day, that we might not burden any of you, while we *preached* to you the gospel of God. . . . For you know how, like a father with his children, we exhorted each one of you and encouraged you and charged you to lead a life worthy of God, who calls you into his own kingdom and glory.

"And we also thank God constantly for this, that when you received the word of God which you heard from us, you accepted it *not as the word of men but as what it really is, the word of God*, which is at work in you believers" (1 Thess. 2:9-13).

Preaching the Word

When Paul preached the gospel, he was preaching not the word of man but the Word of God. The preaching of the gospel is not only a communication of truth about God and the Christian way of life, but also a phenomenon—a holy event—in which the same word that is at work in the hearts of believers is now heard as they listen to the sermon. Preaching is something living and vital, something dynamic and moving. In consideration of this, some have asserted, as does Robert H. Mounce in *The Essential Nature of New Testament Preaching* (p. 152), that in preaching, God reveals Himself, so it can be said that "preaching is revelation"—the revelation of God.

We may consider that point in need of some modification because of its relationship to the doctrine of revelation. But we must not lose its force with respect to the importance of preaching. "Many do not look upon preaching as Christ's appointed means of instructing His people and therefore always to be highly prized. They do not feel that the sermon is the word of the Lord to them and estimate it by the value of the truths spoken; but they judge it as they would the speech of a lawyer at the bar—by the argumentative skill displayed and the power and beauty of the language. The minister is not infallible, but God has honored him by making him His messenger. If you listen to him as though he were not commissioned from above you will not respect his words nor receive them as the message of God. . . .

"We are never to forget that Christ teaches through His servants" (*Testimonies*, vol. 5, pp. 298-300).

Have we lost this concept of preaching? Do we still consider the sermon the "word of the Lord"? Do we believe that in the act of preaching, Christ teaches His people through His servants? Is the Holy Spirit present and active in the sermon—do God and man come together? Something wonderful can happen if preaching is God's appointed means of saving souls. Should we approach the pulpit with the expectation that it will happen?

I miss the attitude of reverence for the pulpit that I was taught as a boy. I remember well the time my parents discovered my sister and me "playing preacher" behind the pulpit. I have never forgotten the lesson applied to my "seat of learning." Our parents taught us that it was dangerous to "fool" with sacred things, and the pulpit was one of these. From the pulpit God speaks to men and women. In the sermon God and man come together.

In *The Art of Illustrating Sermons* Ian Macpherson tells a story that has some bearing upon what we are considering. "Picture an old lady living in London about the middle of last century. Her hero, we will suppose, is the Duke of Wellington, and when we first see her she is sitting in her drawing room, a copy of his biography open in her hands. She is reading the account of the Battle of Waterloo, and as she reflects on the role the duke played in that famous engagement, and on all that the victory he then won has meant for her as an Englishwoman, she is overwhelmed with gratitude and devotion to him. Every now and again she lifts her eyes from the page and looks up at an etching hanging on a wall of the apartment. It is a pen-and-ink drawing of Apsley House, Wellington's London residence; and, as she gazes at it, she says to herself: 'How wonderful to think that the great duke lives there!' Then, all at once, her reverie is broken into by a sharp rap on the door. She rises to respond to it and, when the door is opened, there confronting her in living presence is the duke himself! In a flash, book and building—fascinating though they are—are alike forgotten, for the conqueror meets her face to face!

"Something far more marvelous than that frequently happens in a Christian church. People go there to listen to the reading and exposition of a Book, which tells of a triumph immeasurably surpassing Waterloo, or to gaze with rapture on the stately fabric of some glorious cathedral. And, all at once, there comes a knock on the door of their hearts. There before them is none other than the risen Christ Himself!" (pp. 20, 21).

Will something like that happen when you preach your next sermon? It can. How does that possibility strike you as you prepare the sermon? Are you motivated to do your best? Do you begin your preparation on your knees?

To put it another way, preaching is a means ordained of God whereby God and man come together in communion and communication. As we listen to the Word of God in proclamation, we accept it as the Word of God, which is at work in us (1 Thess. 2:13). The solemnity and beauty of this truth must ever be with us as we go about our task of preaching the Word.

It is in this context, the communion between Heaven and earth, that we receive instruction in the way and will of God. Preaching instructs and informs us with respect to the life that we should live—what we should be, what we should do, and how we should do it. Notice again Paul's words in 1 Thessalonians 2: "For you know how, like a father with his children, we exhorted each one of you and encouraged you and charged you to lead a life worthy of God, who calls you into his own kingdom and glory" (verses 11, 12).

Preaching therefore must involve the proclamation of truth or truths having to do with faith and morals—Christian conduct and lifestyle.

But what truths? Can you proclaim what you *think* is true? No, you must preach what God *says* is true. How do you know what God says? Does God reveal it to you? Yes, God's Spirit prompts you and illuminates your mind, since in the act of proclamation the Word of God is present. But you are not a seer possessing the gift of prophecy. Like all God's people in every generation, you must look to the prophet for a word from the Lord. Ever keep in mind a statement found in the introduction to *The Great Controversy*: "The Spirit was not given—nor can it ever be bestowed—to supersede the Bible; for the Scriptures explicitly state that the Word of God is the standard by which all teaching and experience must be tested" (p. ix).

At this point the Bible becomes indispensable to preaching—so indispensable, in fact, that we can say that *a sermon that is not an exposition of a Bible truth is not a sermon!*

To do all that you have been called upon to do in proclaiming the gospel and instructing men and women in the principles of faith and the practice of obedience—to communicate the great truths that God has revealed to humans through His holy prophets—you must have more than a casual knowledge of the Bible.

A Knowledge of the Word

True, you are not a professional. You may not have had much formal training in Bible study and may never have attended a seminary, but you should have an understanding of the Scriptures that will help in the preparation and delivery of sermons. This chapter and this book will provide some of that understanding.

Certainly you should know how to find book, chapter, and verse in the Bible so you can turn without difficulty to the passage you want. When you cannot find passages referred to in the sermon, you suffer a loss of credibility— your hearers are likely to question the validity of your message. This seems almost too obvious to mention, yet its importance deserves at least a passing comment. Moreover, think of the difficulty imposed upon the preacher who cannot find "texts" in the preparation of the sermon! Acquiring skill in this matter is not difficult. Memorize, in order, the books of the Old and New Testaments, and the rest is a matter of locating chapter and verse by number.

Having found the text, do you know what it *says*? Do you know what it *means*? To do the first, you will need to rely on translations, since you cannot read the Scriptures in the original languages—Hebrew, Aramaic, and Greek. The second involves interpretation.

At this point you again begin to feel your inadequacy. But take heart. Help is available. The Bible, as we all know, has already been translated into English and beyond that into numerous versions. But that of itself poses a problem. Which is the best translation or version?

To begin with, be careful in using one of the modern paraphrases, such as the *Reach Out* Bible or *Good News for Modern Man*. These are good for devotional reading, but they can be misleading because the more the text is paraphrased or put into common language the more it is interpreted, and that, of course, affects its meaning.

There are, however, several good versions. I begin my study with the Revised Standard Version (now newly revised), and then I go to others for comparison. These might be the New International Version or the *New American Standard Bible*, which many scholars consider to be the most accurate translation to date. The King James Version or, more in keeping with today's language usage, the New King James Version is also helpful. Protestants in the English-speaking world were raised and nurtured on the King James Version, which many still love to hear used in preaching because it has that familiar ring, and is, indeed, an excellent representation of the English language. But remember, what you want at this point is the most accurate representation of what the text *says*.

What the text *means* is another matter. You may know what it says, but do you know what it means? The Protestant church has been divided into numerous denominations because, while people may agree as to what the Bible says, they do not all agree as to what it means. What it means is the

14

basis for Bible doctrine. Because of this, a most important discipline in Bible study has been developed—*hermeneutics*. Hermeneutics is simply another word for *interpretation* and is based upon a Greek word found in the New Testament. Luke 24:27, speaking of Jesus, says, "Beginning with Moses and all the prophets, he interpreted [*diermèneusen*] to them in all the scriptures the things concerning himself."

A course in hermeneutics deals with rules for interpretation that go beyond what you are prepared to cope with, but here are a few principles you can follow that are consistent with a Seventh-day Adventist understanding of the Bible as the Word of God.

1. The Bible is the authoritative Word of God in which eternal truths are revealed concerning who He is, who we are, and His purpose for us with respect to our salvation from sin and its curse. This includes a revelation of His will for us as to our relationship to Him and to one another in this life in preparation for immortality in the life to come.

2. The Bible is to be understood literally unless there is adequate reason to understand it otherwise. We know the Bible contains poetry, as in the Psalms; figures of speech, as in Isaiah 55:12 ("The mountains and the hills before you shall break forth into singing, and all the trees of the field shall clap their hands"); allegory, as in Galatians 4:24 ("These women are two covenants"); and symbolic prophecy, as in Daniel and Revelation. But when we go to the Bible for instruction and guidance from the Lord, our first expectation is that He will say what He means and mean what He says. In other words, we believe in the primacy of the literal meaning of Scripture.

3. There is a theological unity in the Bible. The Bible is not a collection of theologies, but contains a consistent theology throughout. This is not to say that its theology is complete in every part or book, or that revelation is not progressive, or that it is free of all paradox and mystery (the finite mind cannot fully comprehend the infinite; therefore God accommodates His revelation to human limitations).

Nevertheless, taken as a whole, the Bible is a true and reliable revelation of God.

4. Because of the unity indicated above, scripture interprets scripture. Not all the truth concerning a doctrine or teaching may be found in one text or scripture portion, but it may be gathered from various scripture portions wherever that truth is revealed. Therefore what may not be clear in one statement may be interpreted or clarified by another passage found elsewhere.

5. To a large degree the Bible is a history book. It tells a story—how the world was created; how God called a people, Israel, to represent Him in the world; how Jesus came into the world to save the world from sin; and how His church was founded to prepare the way for His return.

To understand the Bible, then, it is important to know the story of the Bible and to be aware of the historical, cultural, and social contexts in which its books were written.

6. Every interpretation must have adequate justification. Know why you interpret Scripture the way you do. To help in all this are excellent reference works such as concordances, commentaries, and study guides. Most of you will not have an extensive library containing such works, but all of you should have a set of *The Seventh-day Adventist Bible Commentary* and *Dictionary*, and a set of the Conflict of the Ages Series, by Ellen G. White (*Patriarchs and Prophets*, *Prophets and Kings*, *The Desire of Ages*, *The Acts of the Apostles*, and *The Great Controversy*). Beyond that you may have a number of the other books written by Mrs. White, a good concordance such as Cruden's or Walker's, and a set of commentaries such as *The Interpreter's Bible* or the Daily Study Bible Series, by William Barclay. When working with sources that are not Seventh-day Adventist, you will, of course, evaluate the assertions in terms of your theology and doctrinal convictions and those of the church you serve.

Does the task seem formidable? Have I frightened you more than I have helped you? Perhaps you feel somewhat like the little boy who fell into the molasses barrel. As he came out of the barrel, his whole body covered with sweetness, he started licking the goo dripping from his fingers. Suddenly he stopped, and with a look of utter frustration exclaimed, "My tongue is not equal to the occasion!"

Take heart! God's promises are His enablings. Let me encourage you with some words from the apostle Paul found in 1 Corinthians 2:10-13: "God has revealed to us through the Spirit. For the Spirit searches everything, even the depths of God. . . . So also no one comprehends the thoughts of God except the Spirit of God. Now we have received . . . the Spirit which is from God, that we might understand the gifts bestowed on us by God. And we impart this in words not taught by human wisdom but taught by the Spirit, interpreting spiritual truths to those who possess the Spirit."

Spiritual things are spiritually discerned. When you prepare to preach, you do not prepare alone. The Spirit is present to guide you and to illuminate your mind so that you may understand God's Word. He is as present during the preparation of your sermon as He is when you preach it. Pray, then, for the presence and guidance of the Holy Spirit. Without Him we can do nothing. In Him we can do all things.

2

The Sermon

What is a sermon? Something the pastor preaches on Sabbath morning? That's true, of course, but what is it that is preached on Sabbath morning?

A sermon has been defined as a religious speech or as a religious discourse with parts. Webster defines it as "a discourse delivered in public, usually by a clergyman, for the purpose of religious instruction, and grounded on a passage of Scripture." This is true, and other formal, theoretical definitions might be added. But a much more fruitful understanding comes with the doing. Going through the process of preparing a sermon brings definition and comprehension. What is needed, then, is an "operational" definition of the sermon.

Creating the Sermon

A sermon is not just prepared—it is created. You cannot prepare a sermon in a detached, offhand, dispassionate way. Under the guidance of the Holy Spirit, your whole being is involved. In a special sense, you give birth to the sermon. For that reason, if for no other, the preparation of a sermon is not easy.

While a sermon is a religious speech, or a discourse with parts, or a discourse delivered in public, it is more than that.

And that "more" is apprehended rather than defined. It is something caught rather than taught.

Therefore, preparation of the sermon must begin with prayer. To say this may seem like repeating the obvious, but it bears repeating. An openness to the guidance of the Holy Spirit is indispensable. This is the first principle in preparation.

Clarity and Coherence

While the preparation of a sermon is never easy, it can be made easier with some guidance as to method and technique in the preparation of the sermon as a discourse. Did you ever hear a sermon that fell gelatinously all over the congregation? Gelatinously? Julian Huxley first used the term in reference to the perambulations of an invertebrate sea animal. Halford Luccock in his book *In the Minister's Workshop* sees it as a fit description of a sermon without structure (p. 121).

The problem with a gelatinous sermon is that it lacks clarity and coherence—meaningful coordination. There is, to be sure, a profound mystery in the gospel and in the Bible that no amount of sermonizing can eliminate. However, the object of our preaching is not to compound the mystery and confuse, but to clarify and make what God has said as comprehensible and meaningful as possible.

When Paul was confronted in Corinth with confusion in the communication of the gospel, he wrote: "If even lifeless instruments, such as the flute or the harp, do not give distinct notes, how will any one know what is played? And if the bugle gives an indistinct sound, who will get ready for battle? So with yourselves; if you in a tongue utter speech that is not intelligible, how will any one know what is said? For you will be speaking into the air." "In church I would rather speak five words with my mind, in order to instruct others, than ten thousand words in a tongue" (1 Cor. 14:7-9, 19).

When the hearer says, "I heard you say many good things, but I couldn't follow you; I don't know what you were talking about—what you were getting at or where you were going," the problem is one of clarity and coherence.

If the preacher is to encourage and charge the hearers "to lead a life worthy of God" (1 Thess. 2:11, 12), what is said must not be muddled, ambiguous, or confusing. This is the second principle in sermon preparation. Clarity and coherence should characterize Christian preaching.

Simplicity

Simplicity is one of the keys to clarity. Simplicity, in this context, must not be confused with stupidity, dullness, or crudity. Rather, it should be understood in the sense that Ellen G. White uses the word. In *Gospel Workers*, page 170, she writes, "Ministers should present the truth in a clear, simple manner."

What she means is perhaps best illustrated in the reference she makes to the preaching of Jesus. For example: "In these words [the Sermon on the Mount] spoken by the greatest Teacher the world has ever known there is no parade of human eloquence. The language is plain, and the thoughts and sentiments are marked with the greatest simplicity. The poor, the unlearned, the most simple-minded, can understand them" (*Testimonies*, vol. 5, p. 254).

One of the great challenges in preaching is making the profound simple, making clear to creatures who are finite what the Infinite One has revealed. May it never be said of any of us what one woman said of her pastor: "For six days he is invisible and on the seventh day he is incomprehensible!"

The Precise Word

Jesus "did not use long and difficult words in His discourses; He used plain language, adapted to the minds of the common people" (*Gospel Workers*, p. 169). This should not be taken to encourage indolence in vocabulary development. Although we should use simple words that are commonly understood, we need to use the appropriate word—the word that best expresses the thought. The more words you know, the better able you are to choose the right word to express the thought precisely in the language of the common people.

Language

You will recall that Jesus used plain language. This does not mean that He disregarded the rules of grammar and syntax. His speech was not uncouth just because it was plain. He employed a proper usage of the language of the people. His sentences were uncomplicated and short.

Too often we carry the impression that good grammar and syntax go with sophisticated eloquence but not with plain language. Not so. The rules of grammar and syntax are to make for clarity and precision of expression. This is as important in plain language as it is in the most profound oratory.

Proficiency in the use of language does not come by accident. While it is true that some people have more of a gift for fluency than others, even the gifted must strive for excellence. In this striving, two things bring rich rewards— reading and writing.

Read material that is well written but not difficult and complicated. Read that which impresses you with its simplicity and clarity but which is rich in thought and profound in truth. As you read, be sensitive to that which makes what you read clear and understandable. Notice the choice of words, the way they are put together, the kinds of sentence structure, the effectiveness of good grammar, and the development of the main theme or subject. The more you read, the more you will come to express yourself in a manner similar to that which characterizes the material you have read.

Practice writing what you plan to say. This may be painful, to be sure, but that is all it costs, and the rewards in your ability to use language effectively far outweigh the cost. You need not write out a full manuscript of every sermon you prepare, although you may want to do just that at times (this will be discussed at greater length when we consider the delivery of the sermon). Instead, practice writing only part of the sermon, especially when you find it hard to say what you want to say. Or put words on paper at other times in order to develop skill in the use of language. What is so helpful about writing what you want to say is that you can read and correct what you have written. And that's hard to beat as a learning experience.

How many times have you heard a person say, "I know what I want to say, but I just can't put it into words"? What a tragedy when preachers get into the pulpit and know what they want to say but can't put it into words! Certainly this is one of the cardinal sins, if not a mortal one! If you suffer that kind of dilemma, it would be better for you not to enter the pulpit in the first place.

Building the Sermon

For a sermon to be coherent it must have adequate structure or design. This is true of all speechmaking, whether it be secular or religious. When the sermon is hard to follow or when the message just "tumbles forth," the problem could very well be one of poor structure or no structure at all.

William J. Carl III suggests the reason for this in a book entitled *Preaching Biblically*: "What is at issue here is the almost innate human desire to order experience—to bring order out of chaos in any production of speech, action, music, or light and color. . . .

"Because we desire order and structure, we supply it even if it's not there entirely. We hear a lecture or a sermon, and we unconsciously do our best to put together in our minds what the lecturer or the preacher is trying to say; or we tune out altogether. We try to bring order to sermons that otherwise might be without form, and void" (pp. 122, 123).

Notes thrown together do not make a song. Paint splashed on canvas does not make a picture. Boards, nails, and stone thrown together do not make a house. When we build a house, we organize the materials in such a way that we have rooms with floors, ceilings, walls, windows, and doorways. When it is done well, it not only looks good—it also "works."

So, what are the materials, and how should they be put together when you are building a sermon? To begin with, you should ask yourself two fundamental questions: (1) What am I talking about? and (2) What am I saying about it? In homiletical terms, what you are talking about is called the *theme*, and what you are saying about it is called the *parts*.

For instance, you decide to preach a sermon on the Bible as the Word of God—that's what your sermon is about. But what are you going to say about it? Well, you might say: (1) The Bible is inspired by God. That's the first part, and if that is all you plan to say, then your sermon has one part. But more than likely you will say more than that. Perhaps you will also say: (2) The Bible is a revelation of God. That's the second part. And you might also add: (3) The Bible contains the power of God's Word.

We might outline these thoughts like this:

Theme—The Bible is the Word of God.

Parts— I. The Bible is inspired by God.

       II. The Bible is a revelation of God.

     III. The Bible contains the power of God's Word.

Of course, each of the parts will be fleshed out so that the hearers will know what you mean and better understand each part. But this is essentially what teachers mean when they define a sermon as a discourse with parts.

The first step, then, in preparing a sermon is to ask the two questions: (1) What am I talking about? and (2) What am I saying about it? When words flow from your mouth, you are either talking about something or you are not. If not, you may be making sounds, but you are not talking. If you are talking about something, you are, by the same token, saying something about it. That may be so basic as to seem obvious, but it is surprising how often basics are taken for granted because they seem obvious. Which may be why we hear too much preaching that is made up of a lot of lightning and thunder but signifying nothing. Remember the gelatinous sermon? Like the invertebrate sea animal, it needs a bony structure.

The theme, or what you are talking about, should be

central to the sermon. And everything you say should be related to it. Why? Because the average audience cannot accommodate more than one basic concept in the time ordinarily given to a sermon. Moreover, the preacher cannot adequately develop more than one theme in that amount of time. To burden the mind with too many unrelated ideas at any one time is to create confusion and bewilderment.

Mrs. White speaks to this point in *Testimonies to Ministers*, pages 309, 310: "You have made of none effect many precious ideas, by mixing them with other thoughts which have come to your mind but which had no bearing upon the subject. That which is far from the subject under consideration should find no place in your discourses."

The ideal toward which to strive is that of gathering the whole of your sermon into a topic sentence. When you can summarize in one sentence all that you want to say in the sermon, you have a sermon that—in this respect, at least—has *unity*.

Unity has always been stressed in the classical works on homiletics. In his book *On the Preparation and Delivery of Sermons*, John A. Broadus quotes from Herrick Johnson's *The Ideal Ministry*: "A work of art may express a variety of ideas, but it cannot remain a work of art unless this variety is held together by the unity of a single idea. The sermon, too, may and should present a variety of thoughts; yet it dare not be a barrage of heterogeneous and arbitrarily assembled elements, but must form an organic unity" (p. 97).

M. Reu in *Homiletics* devotes a section to the structure of the sermon. Of first consideration in this section is the element of unity: "The first requirement of the sermon, with regard to structure, is *unity*" (italics supplied). He then goes on to show how unity was emphasized by Fenelon, Vinet, Porter, and Herrick Johnson (pp. 390-414).

I. H. Evans wrote in *The Preacher and His Preaching*: "Every sermon should have unity. By this we mean that from first to last all that is said should be essential to make completeness, wholeness" (p. 172).

Choosing the Theme—You have been asked to preach

next Sabbath. What will you preach about? Or perhaps the question should be: What *should* you preach about? The reason for changing the question is that preaching is a matter of proclaiming not your words, but God's Word.

Preaching begins not with man, but with God. For that reason *you* must begin with God. "Lord, what do You want me to say?" This is the preacher's prayer, and it must ever be so. You should begin your sermon preparation not only on your knees but also with God's Word—the Bible. And as you pray and as you read, you must pray and read in faith. God *will* guide you.

This does not mean that Friday night you will pray for a message to deliver on Sabbath morning. It means that as soon as you learn of your appointment to preach, you will begin talking to God about it. You will begin to listen to God as you read His Word. You will carry the matter on your heart. You will reflect and meditate and brood over it, and as you do so, God will impress you with what He wants you to say. He will not give you the whole sermon ready-made so that all you have to do is open your mouth and out it will come. But He will impress you with the theme or lead you to the text He wants you to proclaim.

Organizing the Parts—Let us assume that the Spirit has impressed you to preach on a great biblical truth, the love of God. What are you going to say about His love? What do you know about it? What does the *Bible* say about it? Do you have any good books or articles that rightly represent what the Bible says about God's love, and from which you can gather good quotations, poems, and illustrations? What has Ellen G. White written on the theme? What experiences have you had that testify to the love of God? (There is no more powerful illustration, persuasion, or argument in favor of the truth of a given theme than your own personal experience.)

As you come upon such materials in the course of your study, gather them all together. They will not be in any order or arrangement, but they will all have to do with the theme—the love of God. The next step is to put them in order. What comes first? What comes last? That you will have to decide. But you are not without help. Rhetorical theory (homiletics) suggests that the parts of a theme or topic may be arranged in various ways—chronologically, episodically, logically, or psychologically.

For instance, matters can be arranged in terms of time sequence. What happens first comes first, and what happens last comes last. Or as in a story, the narrative unfolds by episodes. The beginning of the story comes first, and the end comes last. In dealing with a great concept or truth, reason may call for a certain progression in the unfolding of the truth. Because of logical relationships between one idea and another, reason may require that one idea follow another in logical relationship. Certain occasions, the nature of the audience, or the relationship between the speaker and the audience might also make it more sensible to start with one thought or idea and proceed to the next. In other words, taking into consideration the audience, the circumstances, and the occasion, it might be well to ask the question What is the first thing that will come to the minds of the congregation as I introduce this topic? What will they think about next? By anticipating how the members of the congregation will think as you present the sermon, you can arrange psychologically the parts of the theme.

To explain further, let us suppose that the material you have gathered on the theme of God's love can be organized into four divisions: (1) the love of God and you; (2) the nature of the love of God; (3) the power of the love of God; and (4) the revelation of the love of God. In what order should you arrange these divisions? With this theme, the chronological and episodic order do not seem appropriate.

The logical order might look something like this:

I. The revelation of the love of God

II. The nature of the love of God

III. The power of the love of God

IV. The love of God and you

The psychological might look like this:

I. The love of God and you

II. The power of the love of God

III. The nature of the love of God

IV. The revelation of the love of God

You have two outlines of the theme "The Love of God." In other words, you have a diagram of how different parts or divisions of the theme are arranged according to a certain order. With this outline or diagram you may proceed in greater detail.

So far you have the theme and the main divisions of that theme. Now you need to expand the outline to include the main subdivisions under each main division.

The Love of God

I. The revelation of the love of God (main division)

   A. The revelation in God's Word—the Bible (main subdivision)

   B. The revelation in God's Son—Jesus Christ (main subdivision)

II. The nature of the love of God (main division)

   A. The love of God is selfless (main subdivision)

   B. The love of God is personal (main subdivision)

III. The power of the love of God (main division)

   A. The love of God gave us His Son (main subdivision)

   B. The love of God moves heaven and earth (main subdivision)

IV. The love of God and you (main division)

   A. You may reject the love of God unto death (main subdivision)

B. You may accept the love of God unto eternal life (main subdivision)

Every theme does not need to have four divisions, and every main division does not need to have two subdivisions. The number of divisions may vary. Moreover, each main subdivision may have its own subdivisions (numbered 1, 2, 3, 4, etc.). For instance:

I. Main division
    A. Main subdivision
        1. Subdivision
        2. Subdivision
        3. Subdivision
        4. Subdivision

The point to all this is that the material you gather on the theme should be organized, ordered, and arranged so that the message may not only be heard but understood. This is what is meant by *coherence*—preaching so that the congregation can easily follow your presentation and understand. It all hangs together.

What has been said up to this point may be visualized in a number of ways. First the triangles:

1. You have gathered your material on a particular theme and organized it into four parts represented by four triangles:

2. You have decided the order in which you want to preach these parts—which should come first, which should come second, etc.

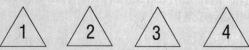

3. You have checked the sermon for unity by asking the following questions: Are the main divisions an elaboration of

28

the theme? Are they part of the theme—do they amplify or modify it in some way? Are the main subdivisions an elaboration of their main division? Are they part of that division—do they amplify or modify it in some way? If so, the triangles will cluster around a common center and look like this:

Some have pictured the sermon as a stream with tributaries running into it. The main stream is the theme, and all the tributaries are a part of it.

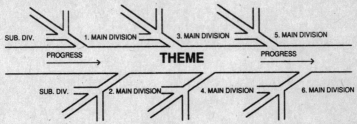

In *Expository Preaching Without Notes*, Charles W. Koller tells of a preacher of pioneer days who introduced one of his sermons as follows: "My text is 'Adam, where art thou?' My sermon has three points: First, Where is Adam? Second, Why was Adam where he was? And third, A few remarks about baptism" (p. 52).

Have you ever heard a sermon like that? Everything was moving along nicely. There was organization and progression, but suddenly the unity broke down. One of the tributaries was not flowing into the stream. It had actually become another stream and was flowing in another direction.

If you are tempted to minimize the importance of structure and arrangement in the sermon, remember this statement by R.C.H. Lenski in *The Sermon*: "Of course, it is true that an excellent sermon may be preached without an excellent inner structure. The preacher may have a fine personality, an excellent voice, natural force, trained eloquence, and a striking way of putting things. Such features may make his sermon excellent. But none of these, not even all of these, features exclude the structural fault. Excellence in one or more points never makes up for inferiority in other points. In fact, a flaw in a great diamond is more deplorable than the same flaw in a cheaper stone" (p. 77).

What if you don't have a "fine personality, an excellent voice, natural force, and trained eloquence"? You can still go a long way in proclaiming the Word of God effectively if what you say makes sense—if it all comes together into a meaningful whole. Unity is to coherence what simplicity is to clarity.

3

Preaching Textually

Up to this point we have considered the building or designing of what is known as a topical sermon: (1) under the impress of the Holy Spirit you have chosen a biblical theme or topic; (2) you have gathered the material into parts or divisions; (3) you have arranged the parts in a certain order or progression; (4) you have checked for unity to be sure that all the parts are an elaboration of the theme or topic. Keep these steps in mind. They are basic to all preaching.

We turn our attention now, however, to another type of sermon, the textual sermon. In terms of the basics with respect to structure, the textual sermon is the same as the topical sermon except for one fundamental difference: the theme, parts, and progression come from a text—a passage of Scripture.

To show how this type of sermon is developed in contrast to the topical, let us suppose that you are reading a passage from Scripture. As you read, you are impressed that a portion of what you are reading would be helpful to the church you serve and would make a good sermon. You feel that the Holy Spirit is speaking to you in the text and that He is impressing you to preach *that* text. Moved by the Spirit, you decide to preach the text the next time you are called upon to preach. But how do you proceed?

1. As with the topical sermon, the textual sermon must have a theme, but now, as indicated above, the theme is provided by the passage itself—the theme of the text will be the theme of the sermon. But how do you identify the theme? By asking the fundamental question What is this text talking about? Answer that question, and you have identified the theme.

2. The textual sermon will also have parts. But here again, the parts will be provided by the text. To identify the parts, ask the other fundamental question What does this text say about the theme?

3. Likewise, the ordering of the parts will be provided by the text in that what it says about the theme will follow a certain progression.

4. Checking for unity is the same as for the topical sermon—all the parts must elaborate or modify the theme.

Perhaps the analysis of a simple sentence will help illustrate. Every complete sentence has a subject and those elements that elaborate or modify the subject. It might be said that the adjectives and verbs tell us something about the subject. In the sentence "God is love," *God* is the subject, and *is love* tells us something about Him. In other words, *God* is the theme and *is love* elaborates on or modifies the theme. If we add to the sentence the word *great*, "The great God is love," we might outline it thus:

God (theme)

I. is great (elaboration or modification)

II. is love (elaboration or modification)

It is obvious, of course, that the shorter the text, the less there will be of elaboration or modification of the theme coming from the passage. This is why a sermon that develops from a one-sentence text is not strongly textual. A much stronger textual sermon results from the use of a paragraph or a larger portion of Scripture.

Since a paragraph is a unit of thought, it usually has a topic sentence and other sentences, clauses, and phrases that elaborate or modify the topic sentence. Thus the topic sentence is the theme, and the other sentences, clauses, and phrases are the parts.

Because a paragraph is a basic unit of thought, it is recommended that when studying the Bible for purposes of preparing a textual sermon, you use a version or translation of the Bible in which the verses are organized into paragraphs. You no doubt have noticed that a number of the newer versions or translations are printed this way.

To further illustrate the building or designing of a textual sermon, let us outline Micah 6:8: "He has showed you, O man, what is good; and what does the Lord require of you but to do justice, and to love kindness, and to walk humbly with your God?" The outline might look like this:

"He has showed you, O man, what is good; and what does the Lord require of you . . . ?" (theme)

I. "To do justice" (elaboration)

II. "To love kindness" (elaboration)

III. "To walk humbly with your God" (elaboration)

Obviously this is just the outline. It must now be filled in with further elaboration or modification. The material may come from a number of sources, such as: (1) the Bible itself; (2) the writings of Ellen G. White; (3) books or commentaries written on the text; (4) life's experiences; and (5) illustrations.

The textual sermon does not exclude the use of other Bible verses or material other than the specific text, but it uses these materials only to elaborate or modify the passage that is the text of the sermon. Since Micah 6:8 is one sentence in length, it can readily be seen that most of the material elaboration will come from outside the text itself. Let us see what happens when we include verses 6 and 7 along with verse 8.

"With what shall I come before the Lord, and bow myself before God on high? Shall I come before him with burnt offerings, with calves a year old? Will the Lord be pleased with thousands of rams, with ten thousands of rivers of oil? Shall I give my first-born for my transgression, the fruit of my body for the sin of my soul?

"He has showed you, O man, what is good; and what does the Lord require of you but to do justice, and to love kindness, and to walk humbly with your God?"

Notice how the theme changes in the longer passage: "With what shall I come before the Lord, and bow myself before God on high?" The topic sentence is a question, and the parts are in response to that question. Notice, too, how the answers to the question are divided into negative and positive. The outline is therefore:

"With what shall I come before the Lord, etc.?" (theme)

    I. Negative responses in the form of oratorical questions:

        A. "Shall I come before him with burnt offerings, etc.?"

        B. "Will the Lord be pleased with thousands of rams, etc.?"

        C. "Shall I give my first-born for my transgression, etc.?"

    II. Positive answer: "He has showed you, O man, what is good:"

        A. "do justice"

        B. "love kindness"

        C. "walk humbly with your God"

To further illustrate the process, let us consider another passage, Romans 5:1-5: "Therefore, since we are justified by faith, we have peace with God through our Lord Jesus Christ. Through him we have obtained access to this grace in which we stand, and we rejoice in our hope of sharing the glory of

God. More than that, we rejoice in our sufferings, knowing that suffering produces endurance, and endurance produces character, and character produces hope, and hope does not disappoint us, because God's love has been poured into our hearts through the Holy Spirit which has been given to us."

The outline of this passage could look like this:

"Therefore, since we are justified by faith" (theme)

I. "we have peace with God through our Lord Jesus Christ." (elaboration)

II. "Through him we have obtained access to this grace in which we stand," (elaboration)

III. "and we rejoice in our hope of sharing the glory of God." (elaboration)

IV. "More than that, we rejoice in our sufferings,"
   A. "knowing that suffering produces endurance,"
   B. "and endurance produces character,"
   C. "and character produces hope,"
   D. "and hope does not disappoint us, because God's love has been poured into our hearts through the Holy Spirit which has been given to us." (elaboration)

In preparing the sermon, the outline would probably be worded something like this:

Theme: The Consequences (or Blessings)
of Justification by Faith

I. We have peace with God.

II. We stand in God's grace.

III. We rejoice in the hope of sharing in God's glory.

IV. We rejoice in suffering because

A. suffering produces endurance
B. endurance produces character
C. character produces hope
D. hope is not disappointed because God's love has been given to us.

This sermon is textual because it preaches the text. The elaboration or modification of the theme is developed in the text. True, other materials will be used to fill out the sermon, but they will all elaborate the theme in keeping with the parts of the theme provided by the text itself. Unity, organization, and progression are present, just as they are in the topical sermon.

Textual Analysis

The key to textual preaching is analysis, the ability to analyze the text in order to identify the parts of the text and their relationship to one another. In many portions of Scripture this is quite simple and straightforward, especially when working with paragraphs or relatively complete units of thought. But there are times when you are impressed by several verses that do not constitute a paragraph. For example, 1 John 1:8-10: "If we say we have no sin, we deceive ourselves, and the truth is not in us. If we confess our sins, he is faithful and just, and will forgive our sins and cleanse us from all unrighteousness. If we say we have not sinned, we make him a liar, and his word is not in us."

You observe readily that the parts of the text are quite apparent: (1) "If we say we have no sin . . ."; (2) "if we confess our sins . . ."; (3) "if we say we have not sinned . . ." But the theme is not so apparent. What is to be done about the theme? You may proceed in one of two ways:

1. You may provide the theme by inference from the text. For instance, the theme of this passage might be "What to do with sin." Should this theme be chosen, the parts might be rearranged to provide a better psychological order.

Theme: What to Do With Sin

I. "If we say we have no sin . . ."

II. "If we say we have not sinned . . ."

III. "If we confess our sins . . ."

When you do this, however, you run the risk of reading something into the text—you might infer something the author never intended. It might be said that you are not faithful to the text.

2. A far better practice than that of inferring the theme from the text is that of determining the theme of the text from its larger context.

Examine the opening chapter of 1 John, and you will see that verses 8-10 are part of a paragraph beginning with verse 5 (see RSV, for example). You will note that verse 5 is a statement followed by a number of verses made up of conditional statements beginning with the characteristic "if." That would make verse 5 the topic sentence or theme of the paragraph: "This is the message we have heard from him and proclaim to you, that God is light and in him is no darkness at all." If this is so, then the "ifs" have something to do with the fact that "God is light."

Theme: God Is Light

I. "If we say we have no sin, we deceive ourselves, and the truth is not in us."

II. "If we confess our sins, *he* is faithful and just, and will forgive our sins and cleanse us from all unrighteousness."

III. "If we say we have not sinned, we make *him* a liar, and *his* word is not in us."

I have emphasized the pronouns in these verses because the antecedent of the pronoun is obviously God, who is spoken of in verse 5, and thus the connection between verses 8-10 and verse 5 is indicated.

But the outline does not yet clearly show how verses 8-10 elaborate verse 5. That is because verses 6 and 7 are missing. If you read the whole paragraph, you observe that verses 6 and 7 help make the transition from verse 5 to verses 8-10: "If we say we have fellowship with him while we walk in darkness, we lie and do not live according to the truth; but if we walk in the light, as he is in the light, we have fellowship with one another, and the blood of Jesus his Son cleanses us from all sin."

While the relationship between God and light is made clear in verses 5 and 7, it is in verse 6 that we see the relationship between darkness and sin. To be in sin is to be in darkness. To have fellowship with God requires that we get rid of sin. The theme of our text might then be: "Fellowship with God, who is light, requires freedom from sin, which is darkness." By shortening the theme, the outline looks like this:

Theme: Fellowship With God
Requires Freedom From Sin

I. "If we say we have no sin . . ."

II. "If we say we have not sinned . . ."

III. "If we confess our sins . . ."

Perhaps you are inclined to ask, "If the above is true, why not preach the whole paragraph rather than just a part of it?" You may indeed! And if so, you might want to rearrange verses 6 to 10 so that progression is from the negative "ifs" to the positive "ifs." The outline for 1 John 1:5-10 could then very well be:

Theme: Fellowship With God
Requires Freedom From Sin Because God Is Light

I. "If we say we have fellowship with him while we walk in darkness, we lie and do not live according to the truth" (verse 6).

II. "If we say we have no sin, we deceive ourselves, and the truth is not in us" (verse 8).

III. "If we say we have not sinned, we make him a liar, and his word is not in us" (verse 10).

IV. "If we confess our sins, he is faithful and just, and will forgive our sins and cleanse us from all unrighteousness" (verse 9).

V. "If we walk in the light, as he is in the light, we have fellowship with one another, and the blood of Jesus his Son cleanses us from all sin" (verse 7).

There should be more preaching that develops longer passages, because this kind of exposition allows the Bible to speak more for itself, it leads the hearers into a deeper understanding of the Word of God, and it presents the message of the Bible in its wider scope—the forest is exposed as well as the trees.

The Homily

There is a kind of textual sermon that is both old and new. It is timeless. It is called the *homily*. In the homily, the sermon develops as a line-by-line, sentence-by-sentence, verse-by-verse commentary. In this way the text is left just as it is. It is not structured or analyzed in order to produce a coherent outline.

Many great sermons have been preached in this way because the passage has a coherence and structure that becomes obvious as the sermon progresses. An argument in favor of this kind of textual sermon is that it is the most faithful to the text, and it is simple—you deal with the text just as it is.

Psalm 24:3-6 might well be preached as a homily:

"Who shall ascend the hill of the Lord? (theme)
And who shall stand in his holy place?
He who has clean hands and a pure heart, (first division)
who does not lift up his soul to what is false,
and does not swear deceitfully.
He will receive blessing from the Lord, (second division)
and vindication from the God of his salvation.
Such is the generation of those who seek him, (conclusion)
who seek the face of the God of Jacob."

But the homily offers some danger. Its apparent simplicity is deceiving. How often have you heard a homily that was nothing more than the King James Version translated into modern speech? Even this need not be done today, with the new "living" versions of the Bible so readily available! A comment by W. E. Sangster in *The Craft of Sermon Construction* is worth noting at this point.

"A generation ago it was not unusual for minor comedians to lampoon this kind of preaching. Avoiding, with proper reverence, any reference to the Bible, they would take their 'passage' from history, or folklore, or nursery rhyme, but imitate with no little skill the unctuous manner and sententious verbosity of the unprepared preacher. I remember hearing one of them 'expound' Old Mother Hubbard. Bits of his droll mimicry float to me down the years.

"'Mother Hubbard, you see, was old; there being no mention of others, we may presume she was alone, a widow—a friendless, old solitary widow. Yet, did she despair? Did she sit down and weep, or read a novel, or wring her hands? No! She *went to her cupboard*. She did not hop, or skip, or run, or jump, or use any other peripatetic artifice; she solely and merely *went* to the cupboard.

"'And why did she go to the cupboard? Was it to bring forth golden goblets, or glittering precious stones, or costly apparel, or feasts, or any other attributes of wealth? *It was to get her poor dog a bone!* Not only was the widow poor, but her dog, the sole prop of her age, was poor too.'

40

"There is enough truth in this foolery to make any serious craftsman solemnly resolve that when, in preaching, he sets out to expound a passage, he will do it with such complete preparation that not even the echo of these caricatures will sound in people's ears" (pp. 73, 74).

Without adequate preparation, a homily can sound very much like that "exposition" of Mother Hubbard.

CHAPTER

4

Other
Options

The previous two chapters have given consideration to basic procedures in sermonic design or construction—some quite simple, some a bit more complex. In all, however, the theme and parts of the sermon have been viewed in terms of the traditional outline. As you begin your preaching ministry, stay with the most simple topical or textual designs. Work with them until they become familiar. Athletes, musicians, artists, all drill themselves again and again on the basics of their particular discipline. They constantly keep returning to them in practice and rehearsal throughout their career.

I remember listening to a sportscaster interviewing a young baseball player who had demonstrated great skill as a hitter in the minor leagues, but when he was called to a major league team and used as a pinch hitter he didn't do well. He was soon traded to another team, on which he played regularly. At once his potential began to be realized. In the interview the sportscaster asked him, "How is it that your hitting has improved so dramatically since being traded?"

He answered, "When not playing regularly, I was bothered by having to analyze each pitch as it left the pitcher's hand. This took only a second, but it threw my timing off. Playing regularly, I react automatically."

The degree to which he had mastery of the basics made the difference.

There are, however, options for sermonic design other than the traditional outline that give flexibility to preaching and the task of preparing the sermon. The gospel is always relevant, but that relevance must not be obscured by locking preaching into some traditional mold that does not allow it to speak meaningfully to people in different ways, under differing social and cultural contexts. Our world keeps changing in many ways, and that includes how we communicate, how we talk to one another. We all recognize the radical change that our modern information media have brought. Hence, we must be flexible.

This is why, when I read in the literature on preaching and communication theory, I keep looking for new ways to shape sermonic material. And when I read Scripture from a homiletical perspective, with the intent to proclaim that Scripture portion, I try to be sensitive to the way that portion wants to be preached.

This does not mean that we forget those basic principles of unity, organization, and progression that make for clarity and coherence. Nor does it mean that we must scrap all the old ways in which sermons have been prepared and preached. We need not "throw the baby out with the bathwater." Rather, we seek a variety of ways, new and old, by which we can preach the gospel with a relevance that brings credibility and conviction.

The following options are only suggestions. You may feel they offer complications that you are not able to handle as a lay preacher. If so, stay with the traditional outline. On the other hand, you may discover something that you find helpful and not too difficult. If so, you have found a way to make your preaching more flexible and, perhaps, more relevant. After all, the more versatile you are in what you do, the more professional you will be even though preaching is not your profession.

Monroe's Motivational Sequence

Alan H. Monroe's motivational sequence, set forth in his

book *Principles and Types of Speech*, has long been considered an effective design for speechmaking when the objective is to persuade. Not that he invented the means or the rules of persuasion, but rather he observed that when good persuasive speeches are made, the five steps in the motivational sequence—attention, need, satisfaction, visualization, and action—are present.

Every student of Scripture and New Testament history knows that the apostle Paul engaged in a great deal of persuasion. He was an evangelist, traveling far and wide to win people to Christ—to persuade them to become followers of Jesus. It should not surprise us, then, to find these steps to persuasion in his writings. When believers need to be corrected or their faith renewed, he uses persuasion. Romans 6:1-14 is an example:

Attention: "What shall we say then? Are we to continue in sin that grace may abound?"

Need: "By no means! How can we who died to sin still live in it? Do you not know that all of us who have been baptized into Christ Jesus were baptized into his death?"

Satisfaction: "We were buried therefore with him by baptism into death, so that as Christ was raised from the dead by the glory of the Father, we too might walk in newness of life."

Visualization (explanation of satisfaction to show assurance of victory in the future): "For if we have been united with him in a death like his, we shall certainly be united with him in a resurrection like his. We know that our old self was crucified with him so that the sinful body might be destroyed, and we might no longer be enslaved to sin. For he who has died is freed from sin. But if we have died with Christ, we believe that we shall also live with him. For we know that Christ being raised from the dead will never die again; death no longer has dominion over him. The death he died he died to sin, once for all, but the life he lives he lives to God. So you also must consider yourselves dead to sin and alive to God in Christ Jesus."

Action: "Let not sin therefore reign in your mortal bodies, to make you obey their passions. Do not yield your members to sin as instruments of wickedness, but yield yourselves to God as men who have been brought from death to life, and your members to God as instruments of righteousness. For sin will have no dominion over you, since you are not under law but under grace."

In this sequence the attention step is the introduction, which should draw attention to the theme—The Christian Life and the Problem of Sinning. This Paul does by asking a rather shocking question. The elaboration of the theme comes in steps 2, 3, and 4—need, satisfaction, and visualization.

The Perry Method

Some years ago John Osborn, who before his death served as president of the Southeastern California Conference, conducted workshops on preaching in which he introduced Adventist preachers to what is called the Perry method. The method is to be found in Lloyd Perry's book *Biblical Preaching for Today's World*, and is designed to help the preacher structure his sermon so that it has good unity and progression. The method employs five steps: subject, theme, proposition, transitional sentence, and major divisions.

The *subject* is the broadest, most inclusive representation of what the sermon is about. It can often be verbalized in one word: sin, obedience, God, salvation, etc.

The *theme* delimits the subject, representing some aspect of it. It is usually impossible to exhaust the subject in one discourse.

The *proposition* qualifies or makes some assertion concerning the theme. (*Proposition* is a term often used in homiletical theory as a synonym for *theme*, since it is a form of stating the theme.) Perry suggests three possibilities: (1) a statement of evaluation or judgment ("Worship is profitable"); (2) a statement of obligation or duty ("We ought to worship God"); (3) a statement of ability or activity without obligation ("We can worship God").

The *transitional sentence* makes the transition from the proposition to the major divisions of the sermon. It contains a key word that names each of the major divisions (a plural noun since there will most likely be more than one division), and an interrogative: why? or how? or what?

The *major divisions* develop the theme of the sermon in terms of the proposition. Notice how this works when applied to a passage such as Ephesians 3:14-19:

Subject: Holiness (what the passage is all about).

Theme: "That you may be filled with all the fulness of God" (verse 19).

Proposition: We can be filled with all the fullness of God (a statement of ability or activity without obligation).

Transitional sentence: We can be filled with all the fullness of God (repeats the proposition).

The interrogative is "how?" which will be represented by the word "by" in order to construct the sentence properly.

The key word is "characteristics," which is determined by the text. In other words, the text mentions certain characteristics of holiness—what it means to be filled with the fullness of God.

Bringing it all together, the transitional sentence becomes: *We can be filled with all the fullness of God by acquiring the characteristics found in Ephesians 3:14-19.*

Main Divisions:

I. First characteristic: "that according to the riches of his glory he may grant you to be strengthened with might through his Spirit in the inner man" (verse 16).

II. Second characteristic: "and that Christ may dwell in your hearts through faith" (verse 17).

III. Third characteristic: "that you, being rooted and grounded in love, may have power to comprehend with all the saints what is the breadth and length and height and depth" (verses 17, 18).

IV. Fourth characteristic: "and to know the love of Christ which surpasses knowledge" (verse 19).

Inductive Preaching

The current literature on preaching emphasizes the inductive method. What this means is best understood perhaps by considering the difference between induction and deduction as two ways of thinking. Inductive thinking draws general conclusions from specific instances and examples. Deductive thinking infers specific conclusions from general presuppositions, axioms, or conclusions that have been drawn from specific instances or examples. In other words, having noticed that every room I have ever seen has at least four walls, I conclude that a room has four walls. This is induction. Since I have concluded that a space enclosed by at least four walls is a room, I am most likely to infer or deduce that the space in which I am standing is a room because it has *four walls*. This is deduction.

The relevance of all this is that these two ways of thinking can offer us two different sermonic designs. If the design of the sermon is drawn from the text, a sermon from Romans 4:1-3, 18-22 would be inductive.

Introduction: "What then shall we say about Abraham, our forefather according to the flesh? For if Abraham was justified by works, he has something to boast about, but not before God. For what does the scripture say? 'Abraham believed God, and it was reckoned to him as righteousness'" (verses 1-3).

For instance: "In hope he believed against hope, that he should become the father of many nations; as he had been told, 'So shall your descendants be'" (verse 18).

For instance: "He did not weaken in faith when he considered his own body, which was as good as dead because he was about a hundred years old, or when he considered the barrenness of Sarah's womb" (verse 19).

For instance: "No distrust made him waver concerning

the promise of God, but he grew strong in his faith as he gave glory to God, fully convinced that God was able to do what he had promised" (verses 20, 21).

Conclusion: "That is why his faith was 'reckoned to him as righteousness'" (verse 22).

If the design of the sermon is drawn from the text, Hebrews 10:19-25 will be deductive.

General conclusion or supposition: "Therefore, brethren, since we have confidence to enter the sanctuary by the blood of Jesus, by the new and living way which he opened for us through the curtain, that is through his flesh" (verses 19, 20). General conclusion or supposition: "And since we have a great priest over the house of God" (verse 21).

Specific inference: "Let us draw near with a true heart in full assurance of faith, with our hearts sprinkled clean from an evil conscience and our bodies washed with pure water" (verse 22).

Specific inference: "Let us hold fast the confession of our hope without wavering, for he who promised is faithful" (verse 23).

Specific inference: "And let us consider how to stir up one another to love and good works, not neglecting to meet together, as is the habit of some, but encouraging one another, and all the more as you see the Day drawing near" (verses 24, 25).

The theme for both passages will either be found in or inferred from the text or from the text's larger context.

The current interest in inductive preaching, however, is not because of its logical qualities, but because of its psychological value. In their *Inductive Preaching*, Ralph and Gregg Lewis argue that the traditional deductive approach in preaching no longer meets the needs of a culture that is largely secular and conditioned by modern communication media, especially television.

"Just as the space age extends the leg by flight, our electronic age extends the brain by computer and word processor, the ear by microphone and the eye by camera. Involvement becomes a way of life, and sensory discovery becomes a primary way of learning" (p. 10).

For them, a key word is "involvement."

"An inductive sermon is one that starts where the people are, with particular elements—the narrative, dialogue, analogy, questions, parables, the concrete experiences—and then leads to general conclusions. In fact, what distinguishes inductive preaching is not so much the ingredients as the use of those ingredients.

"Deductive preaching starts with a declaration of intent and proceeds to prove the validity of what the preacher says is already determined to be true. Inductive preaching, on the other hand, lays out the evidence, the examples, the illustrations and postpones the declarations and assertions until the listeners have a chance to weigh the evidence, think through the implications, and then come to the conclusion *with* the preacher at the end of the sermon.

"Such a process *involves* listeners by giving them a part in the sermon process. It enables them to think along with or even ahead of the preacher. *It involves them*" (p. 43; italics supplied).

The Lewises make a strong case in contending that this is the way Jesus customarily taught the people—through parable. However, they rightly state that Jesus did use deduction and that their book "is no plea to neglect or eliminate the declaring of God's Word, but rather an urging to incorporate additional learning opportunities that can amplify the impact of our preaching by increasing the involvement of our hearers" (p. 30).

And further: "Inductive preaching can't promise to be a total substitute for our existing sermons; it might better serve as a supplement for existing strengths and skills" (p. 32).

Their book contains many illustrations of structures based upon the inductive approach. One that shows the difference between inductive and deductive is found on page 82:

INDUCTIVE	DEDUCTIVE
Illustration	I. Introduction
Statistics	II. Central Idea
Main head A	A. Main head
Illustration	1. Statistics
Instance	2. Illustration
Instance	B. Main head
Main head B	1. Instance
Quotation	2. Instance
Instance	3. Illustration
Subhead 1	C. Main head
Illustration	1. Subhead
Subhead 2	Illustration
Main head C	2. Subhead
Central Idea	III. Conclusion

The Sermon as Story

Any consideration of sermonic design or structure today must not overlook the more recent emphasis upon the sermon as story. Whether or not one agrees with all the assumptions and presuppositions of "theology as story"—from which story preaching got its impetus—the story mode is a structural reality in Scripture. In fact, for the most part, the Bible is a story book. It is the story of Israel in the Old Testament, and of Jesus in the New Testament.

There is the parable sermon and the story sermon in which the whole sermon consists of telling a story. This is a very effective mode in communication and carries with it an internal dynamic and progression. Episode follows episode, suspense follows suspense, until the climax is reached, holding the interest of the hearers and capturing their empathy so that the message is "caught" with meaning and force.

But to tell a parable or a story for 15 or 20 minutes and keep the interest of the congregation, while at the same time making the message clear, takes some doing. It takes special skills that not all preachers possess. (Although serious study and training will help, the ability to tell a good story is basically a gift.)

Given today's orientation to multimedia communication, the sermon must come alive. In this respect, the more recent literature on preaching as story telling is helpful.

Milton Crum's *Manual on Preaching* offers some exciting possibilities. He sees sermon development in terms of "process" through *situation, complication,* to *resolution.* Five dynamic factors give this process vitality:

1. *Symptomatic behavior*—a description of some commonly experienced behavior that needs to be changed by the gospel

2. *Root cause*—of the symptomatic behavior

3. *Resulting consequences*—of the symptomatic behavior

4. *Gospel content*—the word from God that offers an alternative to the old ways of believing and perceiving

5. *New results*—which follow the new way of believing and perceiving

Interestingly enough, though not surprisingly, this process can be found in Scripture. For instance, 1 Corinthians 15:

Situation: *Symptomatic behavior*—verse 12: "Now if Christ is preached as raised from the dead, how can some of you say that there is no resurrection of the dead?" (This is the human tendency to doubt the supernatural—the wisdom and power of God.)

Complication: *Root cause*—verses 33, 34: "Do not be deceived: 'Bad company ruins good morals.' Come to your right mind, and sin no more. For some have no knowledge of

God. I say this to your shame."

Resulting consequences—verses 13-19: "But if there is no resurrection of the dead, then Christ has not been raised; if Christ has not been raised, then our preaching is in vain and your faith is vain. We are even found to be misrepresenting God, because we testified of God that he raised Christ, whom he did not raise if it is true that the dead are not raised. For if the dead are not raised, then Christ has not been raised. If Christ has not been raised, your faith is futile and you are still in your sins. Then those also who have fallen asleep in Christ have perished. If for this life only we have hoped in Christ, we are of all men most to be pitied."

Resolution: *Gospel content*—verses 20-23: "But in fact Christ has been raised from the dead, the first fruits of those who have fallen asleep. For as by a man came death, by a man has come also the resurrection of the dead. For as in Adam all die, so also in Christ shall all be made alive. But each in his own order: Christ the first fruits, then at his coming those who belong to Christ."

New results—verse 58: "Therefore, my beloved brethren, be steadfast, immovable, always abounding in the work of the Lord, knowing that in the Lord your labor is not in vain."

The theme for this sermon is found, of course, in the "situation"—the symptomatic behavior. The elaboration of the theme follows through the other four dynamic factors.

Another source of help in the task of story preaching is Eugene Lowry's *Homiletical Plot*. Lowry's plot or process comes through analogy with drama. The unfolding of the drama is the unfolding of the plot. He says: "Because a sermon is an *event-in-time*—existence in time, not space—a process and not a collection of parts, it is helpful to think of sequence rather than structure. I propose five basic sequential stages to a typical sermonic process. . . . The stages are: (1) upsetting the equilibrium, (2) analyzing the discrepancy, (3) disclosing the clue to resolution, (4) experiencing the gospel, and (5) anticipating the consequences" (p. 25).

This process may also be found in Scripture: Galatians 4:1-7 is an example.

Upsetting the equilibrium: "I mean that the heir, as long as he is a child, is no better than a slave, though he is the owner of all the estate" (verse 1).

Analyzing the discrepancy: "But he is under guardians and trustees until the date set by the father. So with us; when we were children, we were slaves to the elemental spirits of the universe" (verses 2, 3).

Disclosing the clue to the resolution: "But when the time had fully come, God sent forth his Son, born of a woman, born under the law, to redeem those who were under the law, so that we might receive adoption as sons" (verses 4, 5).

Experiencing the gospel: "And because you are sons, God has sent the Spirit of his Son into our hearts, crying, 'Abba! Father!'" (verse 6).

Anticipating the consequences: "So through God you are no longer a slave but a son, and if a son then an heir" (verse 7).

It should be noted that the theme is in the last section of this construction rather than the first—What It Means to Be a Son of God.

Both processes illustrated above work very well with

narrative portions of Scripture—historical narrative, biography, parable, etc. I have intentionally applied them to non-narrative passages to show that they are not limited to just storytelling. The process can bring the dynamics of the story to preaching generally, while at the same time giving the sermon a shape that keeps it from falling gelatinously all over the place. If you wish to enrich your ministry by understanding the processes more fully, read and study the books mentioned.

5

Starting, Stopping, and Opening the Windows

An airplane can be perfect in all its parts. The body, the wings, the engines, and the tail section can be perfectly assembled ready for takeoff, but it will go nowhere until it takes off. Perhaps you know the frustration of sitting on the runway in a loaded plane, anticipating a takeoff that doesn't happen. For some reason, the flight is delayed. We don't build airplanes to sit on runways!

So it is with the sermon. All the parts may be assembled and well developed, but sermons are not prepared in order to sit on the runway. Sermons are prepared so that they can be preached, and that means getting off the ground. And this is important because, as with airplanes, the sermon can crash on takeoff.

The Introduction

In preaching, as in public speaking, that part of the sermon that gets it off the ground is called the introduction. Somehow, in some way, you have to get started. How is this to be done?

First of all, to state the obvious, the introduction should introduce the hearers to what you will be talking about. But beyond that, it should get attention and arouse interest. This is critical, because during the first two to three minutes of your sermon you have the unsolicited attention of your congregation. They are looking at you to see what you look like, wondering what you are going to do, and listening to hear what you have to say. If you don't take advantage of that attention by interesting them in your sermon at this point, you may not get their attention again. This is what we mean when we say the sermon may crash on takeoff.

Second, there is no rule that says how long or how short the introduction should be or what it should consist of. This is a judgment you must make based upon your knowledge of the subject and the needs and interests of the congregation. Of course, the introduction is too long if it leaves insufficient time for the preaching of the sermon itself. It is too short if it doesn't say enough to fulfill its purpose. But beyond that, you must decide.

There are different kinds of introductions:

The story—People are usually interested in stories. "Jim was a boy, about 16 years of age, who had never been more than five miles from home . . ."

The statistic—Statistics are informative and therefore interesting. "Did you know that the most valuable patent ever issued—No. 174,465—went to Alexander Graham Bell?"

The statement that upsets the equilibrium—How it will be resolved holds interest. "Fathers are not fathers just because they have children."

The question—Suggests that an answer is forthcoming. "Do you know the difference between *sin* and *rebellion*?"

Humor—That which draws a chuckle relaxes and entertains as well as interests. "When they asked 'silent' Calvin Coolidge, former president of the United States, what the preacher had preached about that Sunday morning, he answered, 'Sin.' When they asked him what the preacher had said about it, he answered, 'He was against it.'"

An introduction must not be confused, however, with what some have called an icebreaker. A guest speaker, especially, may need to build a bridge to his audience. The atmosphere needs to be relaxed, and both speaker and audience need to become comfortable and feel good about each other. This can be accomplished by humor, a story, a personal experience, or identifying with the congregation on some particular attitude, point of view, or national, ethnic, or social pride or value. Such comments may have nothing to do with what the preacher is going to talk about. They are aimed at simply breaking the ice. This is not the introduction to the sermon, but it is followed by the introduction.

One of the most critical parts of the introduction is the transition from it to the first major part of the sermon or to the proposition or theme. Many times an introduction fails because it doesn't point properly. Remember, the introduction gains the attention and interest of the hearers in what is to follow. When the hearers have to ask "What did that have to do with what he/she is talking about?" the introduction has failed. If necessary, be explicit about that connection. Tell the congregation how that introduction is related to what follows. To be sure, the best introductions do not need that kind of explanation, and we need to guard against insulting the intelligence of the congregation, but clarity is better than confusion when such relationships are in doubt.

The Conclusion

Just as a sermon must get off the ground, so it must land. As there is a beginning, so there is an ending. This is traditionally referred to as the conclusion. That term may be a bit misleading, because a sermon or other type of speech may not have a conclusion. That does not mean it goes on forever, but rather that the nature of the sermon is such that it does not need to make a general or specific inference based upon what has been said, or draw a conclusion from the evidence provided. The sermon may have developed in such a way that the last point made should, indeed, be the last point made. To say more would be superfluous. Here, again, you have to be the judge. But by all means, quit talking and sit down when you are through.

Did you ever hear a preacher say "Now in conclusion," and then keep talking for another 15 minutes? Or did you ever hear him or her come in for the landing and then decide to circle the field one more time? Or worse yet, come in as if to land several times before actually landing? Architects should design trapdoors behind pulpits for such times so that these preachers can be removed quickly and with finality!

Like the introduction, there are no rules for what the end or the conclusion to the sermon should consist of, or how long it should be. The sermon may conclude with a story, a quotation, a question (the answer to which has usually been made obvious by the sermon), or a genuine conclusion or summing up. This summing up is often called a "recapitulation." There is often no better way to end a sermon than by repeating the headings or directional sentences to each of the major divisions of the sermon in the order that they were presented. If what you have said in each division is clear, and even more so if the conclusion to each division has been clearly stated, a repeating of each at the close of the sermon is an adequate and helpful ending. In the words of the old adage: "Tell them what you are going to tell them, tell them, tell them what you told them, and sit down!" Or to put it more crudely: "Stand up, speak up, and shut up!"

Be careful of trite endings such as "My prayer for you is . . ." This is often redundant. The sermon has really ended, but then comes the ignition run-on as in an automobile after the key has been turned off. Pious platitudes are just that, pious platitudes.

Actually, in almost every sermon there is the psychological ending. You come to the point when to say more diminishes the effectiveness of the sermon. You feel this is the moment to quit. Perhaps it is after the reading of a poem, or the telling of a moving narrative. Don't say another word. You will spoil it if you do.

This is not to say that the feeling suddenly comes in the preaching of the sermon. More than likely it will come in the preparation, especially if you prepare carefully and well. And your sensitivity to this feeling will grow with experience.

Opening the Windows

To inform the congregation concerning the truths of

God's Word is one thing. To show their relevance—their importance and significance—is another. True, most people go to church on Sabbath morning feeling the need to hear the Word of God. They may believe that it is important for them as they are confronted daily by the world, the flesh, and the devil. They want to be victorious Christians, and they trust that listening to the sermon will help. But it is possible for them to wonder, having heard the sermon, just how what they have heard should be applied, its meaning for them in today's context.

When, upon hearing the sermon, the hearer asks the question "So what?" something is radically wrong. The preacher failed in some way to apply the truth proclaimed—to give it boots and make it walk. We say the message was irrelevant.

One of the chief ways to effect relevance is through illustration. Illustrations have been referred to as windows in the sermon. They let in light and broaden the vision of the hearers. They contribute greatly to clarity, one of the basic characteristics of good preaching. In *The Art of Illustrating Sermons* Ian Macpherson says: "To begin with their most obvious function, illustrations can help us make our meaning plain. Clarity is a first essential in preaching, and word-paintings are of high value because they can assist us to be clear" (p. 13).

Illustrations are necessary in all manner of discourses. In preaching, the necessity is greater because, more often than not, the subject matter is abstract rather than concrete. Jesus recognized this when He taught in parables. His burden was to clarify and apply the great truths of the kingdom of God. He talked about such things as truth, love, purity, holiness, and how we ought to live as children of God. In addition, He talked about God, the Holy Spirit, heaven, hell, angels, and demons. All this He sought to clarify by using illustrations and parables.

Macpherson suggests other functions that a sermon illustration may fulfill in addition to making the meaning plain. One of them, "bring a sermon down to earth," reinforces what was said earlier about application and relevance. An illustration can turn a "So what?" into a "Now I see!"

Haddon Robinson, in a book entitled *Mastering Contemporary Preaching*, says, "To make a principle come to life—to show how it can be applied—we need to give specific real-life examples, illustrations that say, 'Here is how someone faced this problem, and this is what happened with her'" (p. 61).

But for many a young preacher—including the church elder, who does not claim to be a preacher—the use of illustrations in a sermon constitutes a major problem. The first question—the one most often asked—is Where can one find them; where do sermon illustrations come from?

It might help to consider first the kinds of illustrations that may be used. One could look long and find nothing if one did not know what to look for. W. E. Sangster, in *The Craft of Sermon Illustration*, pages 26-45, discusses nine kinds of illustrations:

1. *Figures of speech*: "His eyes were pools of anger and confusion" (metaphor).

2. *Analogy*: "The water was as clear as crystal" (simile).

3. *Allegory*: "The two humps on the camel are the two branches of government."

4. *Fable*: "Like Jack and the beanstock . . ."

5. *Parable*: "A sower went forth to sow . . ."

6. *Historical allusion*: "You may recall when Abraham Lincoln gave the Gettysburg Address . . ."

7. *Biographical incident*: "When John Wesley heard of the death of George Whitefield . . ."

8. *Personal experience*: "I was standing at the foot of Niagara Falls when . . ."

9. *Anecdote*: "She was on her way to see St. Paul's Cathedral in London . . ."

Illustrations may be found in many places. They may be found in what you read—books, magazines, and papers. Many will come from personal experience. Life is filled with lessons to be learned if only you are alert and aware, and convinced that such is the case. Books of illustrations have been published. Some are better than others, but I have not found them too helpful. They are "canned" illustrations, and sound that way unless used with some skill.

The ability to see sermon illustrations in everyday life is called the homiletic bias. If you have a homiletic bias, you will see illustrations of great truths all about you—in the comment of a child, in the flight of a bird, in the miracle of electronic communications, in a discussion between friends, in reflection upon your own thoughts and reactions to life situations.

Sermons that I have heard or read have been among my best sources for sermon illustrations. I find it easier to use an illustration gleaned from this source because I have heard it or read it in context. I see how it is used to make the point. Which introduces the subject of making the point. An illustration is used to make a point, to clarify a truth. If the illustration makes no point, it is confusing rather than clarifying, distracting rather than illuminating.

I remember a student who came to me one day filled with joy because of a *great* sermon illustration he had heard. He related the story with much enthusiasm and quite a bit of effectiveness. My first reaction upon hearing the story was one of agreement. It was a *good* story. But then I asked, "What was the point of the story—what did it illustrate?" The student's countenance fell a bit, and he looked at me wonderingly. He couldn't remember. The point had escaped him. Great story—but to what point? Sometimes the story can be so dramatic that it ceases to be a useful illustration—we are so enthralled by the story that we miss the point. In such cases, it takes some skill for the preacher to make sure the hearers do not miss the point. Illustrations must illustrate.

While illustrations are windows, there are other means by which what is preached may be made relevant. The preacher may, at some time in his sermon, deliberately ask the question "Now what does this all mean to you and me?" In answering the question, the truths proclaimed are applied so that the hearers will see the meaning in terms of how they are to respond to God's Word. Of course, the answer may be by means of an illustration, but not necessarily so. Such deliberate applications, including the use of illustrations, may come at the end of each major division of the sermon, or at the close of the sermon during the summing up, recapitulation, or conclusion.

Of course, the element of application in a sermon, like making the point in an illustration, may be so obvious that deliberate application is distracting and insulting to the intelligence of the hearers. Good common sense and experience will help you know when this is true. When preparing your sermon, listen to yourself, put yourself in the position of the hearer. This will help you sense the presence or absence of application.

The question of application is addressed by Robinson in this way: "For me, though, the greater danger lies in the opposite direction—in spending too much time on explanation and not going far enough into application. After preaching I've often come away feeling, *I should have shown them in a more specific way how to do this*. It is difficult for our listeners to live by what they believe unless we answer the question 'How?'" (*Mastering Contemporary Preaching*, p. 61).

Since an illustration is often a story, a point or two about telling a story may be helpful:

1. Get into the story. Come alive. Live it; feel it; dramatize it. Watch a child tell a story that excites him or her. Deadpan? No way! Here's an opportunity to get away from your notes (or whatever) and communicate directly and dynamically with your congregation.

A word of caution is needed, however, because being melodramatic (sensational to the point of being ludicrous) is counterproductive. But the opposite is also counterproductive and is, unfortunately, more often the rule rather than the exception.

2. Don't overtell the story. There is the danger of getting bogged down in the details. Clear, crisp description is exciting, but long, drawn-out details are distracting. Let the

mind of the hearer fill in the details as you tell the story. Keep the story moving—action holds interest. Paint the background in broad sweeping strokes. Save the details for the heart of the story. This takes some skill, since it is not always easy to know just what to include and what to omit. You may not be a gifted storyteller, but you can be more effective by keeping some basic principles in mind. Here again you can learn a great deal by observing and listening to good models. Take note the next time you hear a story told well. What made it so good?

Illustrations are a great help in holding attention. They can keep a sermon from sagging into dullness. But more important, they help the hearer see the truth.

CHAPTER

6

Preaching the Sermon

We deal now with matters that have to do with preaching the sermon that you have prepared. This is where the rubber hits the road. Preparation is one thing, delivery is another. The best-prepared sermon goes nowhere unless it is delivered well. This is not to suggest that you must be a fluent orator. Some have a gift for words, others do not. But you can, by observing some basic techniques, be an effective communicator of the gospel.

Preaching Directly and Dynamically

One of your first concerns should be to preach directly and dynamically. This does not mean you must preach bombastically, with overly dramatic voice and sensational body language. You are not an actor. Anything that smacks of affectation in the pulpit detracts from the sermon. Sangster is right when he says in *The Craft of Sermon Illustration*: "You can't in preaching produce the impression that you are clever and that Christ is wonderful" (p. 111).

To achieve direct dynamic preaching as it is here intended, you should first of all let yourself feel the moods in the sermon as you preach it. If you do not feel strongly and deeply about what you are preaching, you will not preach with intensity or conviction. But if you do feel strongly and deeply about it, you should let yourself feel that way when you preach it. Notice, I said "Let yourself feel." Too often, what happens when you get in front of people to address them is a stage fright that won't let you feel anything but fear. Here is where faith and trust come to your aid. Remember, you are not on your own. Since the Holy Spirit has guided you in your preparation, He will not forsake you in your preaching. Learn to lean upon Him. This is not easy, but it can be done, and experience will help. The more you preach, as with any other skill, the more secure you feel when doing it. Only as you trust and relax can you feel the moods of the sermon while you are preaching.

Second, let yourself give expression to these feelings. Notice that I again said "Let yourself." You will not sound affected or phony if you let it happen rather than make it happen. Notice how you express yourself with feeling when you are talking to a friend in conversation. Let that same thing happen while you are preaching. The only difference is that you are speaking to a group of friends instead of just one. I have always been amazed at how expressive my students are when communicating with each other in the hallway. Somehow that all falls away when they get up to preach a sermon in class.

Did you ever notice the difference between the delivery of the preacher when he or she is telling a story to the children during storytime and when he or she gets back into the pulpit to preach the sermon? Notice next time how everyone listens while he or she is talking to the children and how that changes when he or she stands behind the pulpit. Why not keep the same dynamic in the pulpit that you manifest when talking to people under other circumstances?

"Easier said than done!" you say.

Of course, but it is worth the effort. Work on it!

Another factor affecting direct dynamic communication is good eye contact. There is power in the eyes. When you speak to a person with conviction and in earnest, you look that person in the eye. No successful salesman looks out the window when closing the sale. Look at your congregation while you preach. Don't try to look at everyone at the same time. You can't do it. If you try, you will end up looking at no one. Look right at people sitting before you—first one, then another. Don't look at any one person too long so as to embarrass him or her, but on the other hand, don't flit with your eyes from one to another. Look at people in different parts of the congregation, even in the balcony if there is one. Notice how, when you look first at one person and then another in any part of the church sanctuary, you are looking at everyone. It is called "polarization." You polarize the whole congregation when you look at one and then another as you speak. And do it at random, not by design. Let it happen. It will excite you as you see and feel the dynamic that begins to take place. At first, it might also scare you (we are such self-conscious wimps!), but with experience this too will pass.

But of course, in order to look at people while you are speaking, you must remember what you have planned to say. This is where the rub comes. How can you prepare your sermon so that it is easier to remember?

It depends, first of all, on how well you have designed your sermon. That is why so much attention has been given in this book to sermonic design. You can fix a design in your mind much easier than you can page after page of sermon manuscript. This is not to say that you should not write out a full sermon manuscript or preach from one. There are many effective manuscript speakers, but their sermons are more easily remembered because they are well designed. It takes a special gift to remember a manuscript word for word. Even then, unless it is delivered with exceptional skill, the hearers can tell that it has been memorized, which diminishes its effectiveness. The manuscript can always be read, of course, but then eye contact suffers, and few people read well in public. To do so takes special training and skill. Moreover, the distractions of reading are more pronounced when speaking to a small congregation than to a large one.

Second, memory of what you plan to say comes much more easily if you write in oral style rather than written style.

That means write as you speak. Don't write an essay; write a sermon. When speaking, you tend to use shorter sentences than when writing. You also tend to connect phrases together rather than complete sentences, and you tend to inject words and phrases for the sake of emphasis by way of repetition and to express feelings. For example: "You didn't hear me, of course you didn't, you were not interested!" Or: "Look at it. Look again and again; see if you can tell the difference."

In *Preaching for Today*, Clyde Fant suggests that we speak in thought blocks rather than paragraphs, and that each thought block begins with a directional phrase or sentence (p. 120). Write in thought blocks rather than traditional paragraphs. An excellent way to develop an oral style of writing is to speak what you want to say into a tape recorder and then transcribe from the tape just the way you said it. Correct only grammatical and syntactical errors.

Third, outline the sermon in keeping with its design, keeping in mind the two fundamental questions "What am I talking about?" and "What am I saying about it?" Use words, phrases, and symbols that easily come to mind. The outline should include, at least: (1) the topic, theme, or proposition stated as succinctly as possible; (2) the introduction stated succinctly or in outline; (3) the headings or directional sentences of the major divisions; (4) the headings or directional sentences of the main subdivisions; (5) the key word(s) or directional phrase of each transition between the major divisions; (6) the conclusion stated succinctly or in outline. If you fix these six elements in mind, they provide hooks upon which to hang what you want to say and enable you to say what you planned to say without remembering word for word. If you have "packed" the sermon well in preparation, it is simply a matter of "unpacking" it in delivery. In *A Primer for Preachers* Ian Pitt-Watson tells of how, because of time constraints, "I had to invest most of my time in knowing exactly what I was going to say; but precisely how I was going to say it would have to wait until, within the context of worship, I faced my congregation. The result was undoubtedly a loss in economy and precision of expression, but the trade-off in terms of immediacy and spontaneity more than compensated for the loss" (p. 85).

You may find this approach most helpful as you seek to communicate directly and dynamically.

In the last analysis, however, what you take into the pulpit must be *yours*. It may not make sense to anyone else. It may be a cross of some kind between an outline and a manuscript. Above all else, it should be easy for you to use and prepared in such a way as to help *you* keep in mind what you plan to say. I generally prepare an outline, with certain parts of the sermon written in full, including quotations that I plan to read. The congregation will usually not take exception to your reading portions that you want expressed in a precise and certain way or quotations, which they don't expect you to memorize. Remember, what you want to avoid is the loss of direct, dynamic communication.

Just a few words about transitions. Moving from one part of the sermon to another is made much easier and is more easily remembered (as indicated above) if the parts are connected by good transitions. For example, between two major divisions you might say "Having become aware of the justice of God, let us turn our attention to God's mercy and compassion." The sky is the limit. There are many ways of creating good transitions. And while it helps you fix the sermon in your mind, it is also helpful for the hearers because they are hearing the sermon not reading it. When reading something, you can always go back and reread to pick up the thread of thought or note relationships between ideas or concepts, but in oral communication you hear it and it is gone. If you miss it, you may never catch it again unless the speaker repeats it or helps you recall through a recapitulation in transition.

Speech Production

Adequate attention must be given to proper speech production. Ellen G. White has written: "In all our ministerial work, more attention should be given to the culture of the voice. We may have knowledge, but unless we know how to use the voice correctly, our work will be a failure" (*Gospel Workers*, p. 86).

"Ministers and teachers should discipline themselves to articulate clearly and distinctly, allowing the full sound to every word. Those who talk rapidly, from the throat, jumbling the words together, and raising the voice to an unnaturally high pitch, soon become hoarse, and the words spoken lose half the force which they would have if spoken slowly, distinctly, and not so loud" (*ibid*., p. 91).

While it is impossible, of course, to provide a full treatment of the subject of voice and articulation in this chapter, some basic guidelines may be helpful. (For those who would like to pursue the subject further, much excellent help is available in this area. Under the general heading of speech, a number of books may be found in almost any public library on either voice and articulation or voice and diction.)

Proper Breathing: Since the sounds of speech are produced by air passing over the vocal chords or bands in the larynx, proper breathing is very important. But too often, when a conscious effort is made to breathe deeply, the shoulders are thrown back and raised in an effort to enlarge the rib cage and expand the lungs. Not only is this practice unnatural; it is also ineffective. Breathing from the diaphragm is natural and much more effective because it allows for control in breathing, which is essential to proper voice production. How to breathe properly is often a matter of learning good habits through practice and discipline.

Virgil A. Anderson suggests the following helpful exercises:

"1. Lie flat on your back in a relaxed condition and note the activity in the middle portion of your body as you breathe quietly. Place a book on your stomach and watch it rise and fall as you inhale and exhale. Get the 'feel' of this method of breathing.

"2. Stand in an easy position with your back flat against the wall and with the edge of a book pressed against your stomach three or four inches below the end of the sternum. Exhale fully, forcing as much air as possible out of the body.

If necessary, help this process along by pressing in on the book. When as much air as possible has been expelled, begin to inhale slowly, pushing the book away from you in the process by expanding that portion of the body against which it rests. Feel the action of the diaphragm pressing the upper viscera out against the book. This exercise should be continued at intervals . . . until breathing has become easy and under perfect control.

"3. Assume an easy standing position, but not against the wall this time, weight on the balls of the feet, chin in, chest up though not held rigid. Place the hands across the stomach with the fingertips touching at the position where the book was placed before. Breathe easily and quietly, feeling the expansion in front and at the sides. Take care to see that the upper portion of the chest remains passive and relaxed" (*Training the Speaking Voice*, pp. 40, 41).

On the subject of breath control, Anderson says: "One of the most serious faults in the management of the breath for voice production is that of allowing a portion of it to escape before vocalization has begun. A person may take a good, full breath, but if he loses half of it before beginning to speak, he may find that he must replenish the supply in the middle of a thought-group or finish the phrase under strain by squeezing out the last bit of air within the lungs. The breath should not be wasted; it should be retained and used only as it is needed to sustain phonation. Since even a passive exhalation resulting merely from relaxation causes the breath to be expelled with considerable force . . . the process of controlling exhalation for speech becomes to a certain extent a control of relaxation of the diaphragm and other muscles involved. Control thus involves a process of gradually parceling out the breath as it is needed to maintain speech" (*ibid.*, p. 42).

You cannot be heard clearly unless you speak with sufficient force. Unfortunately, when most people attempt to speak more loudly, they tend to raise the pitch of their voice rather than increase the force. Force in speech is a matter of breath control. As the air passes over the vocal cords with great force, the volume of sound is increased. It naturally follows, then, that deeper breathing and greater volume go together. While it may be observed that a change in pitch takes place as the volume increases, it must be remembered that the change in pitch alone does not produce the change in volume. This is not to say, however, that the pitch of the voice is not important. It is intended, rather, to clarify the relationship between pitch and force.

Pitch: Speaking with the voice at an abnormal pitch accomplishes two things. First, it annoys the hearer, which affects clarity adversely; and second, it tires the speaker by placing him or her under unnecessary strain. It is important that the preacher learn to speak at what is known as optimum pitch. With respect to vocal pitch, Anderson writes: "While there is no general basic level of pitch that is best for all voices, there is within the range of each one a pitch at which that voice performs with maximum loudness being attained with a minimum of effort, and the tone at that point being most rich, full, and resonant. This level, which is often referred to as the 'optimum pitch,' will be found to vary in different individuals because, it is believed, it results from a number of anatomical factors, one of them being the structure of the larynx itself, which, . . . is instrumental in determining the pitch possibilities of the individual voice. It is probable that optimum pitch is also importantly related to resonance, being the pitch at which the resonators of the voice function with maximum effectiveness" (*ibid.*, p. 79).

To find your optimum pitch, Anderson recommends: "Using a piano if possible, sing down the musical scale with a sustained a (as in father) or o, beginning with a tone that is easy for you, until you reach the lowest limit of your range. Now, beginning with this lowest note, sing back up the scale until you reach a point some three or four full steps (whole notes) above this lowest limit. This should be close to your optimum pitch.

"As an example, if you are a man and find that the lowest note you can sustain effectively is F below C, then your theoretical optimum pitch would be at about B or C—three to four notes above your lowest note" (*ibid.*, p. 84).

To a local elder or lay preacher this instruction about breathing and pitch may seem too technical and bothersome. But in the light of the guidance given by Ellen White, can such matters be ignored? When called upon to stand in the pulpit and speak for God, or to let God speak, can we afford to do less than our very best? Do people sit and suffer while you preach? They need not. A little practice and application of the suggestions made here can help increase your effectiveness.

Articulation: Did you ever hear a person speak who sounded as though he or she were trying to talk through a mouthful of pebbles? The speech wasn't clear, was it? Either the person *couldn't* articulate well or *didn't* because of sloppy speech habits. When a speech impediment affects the speech mechanism, the problem is serious indeed—there may be no easy solution. But when muffled, mumbled, or sloppy speech results from faulty speech habits, correction is a matter of overcoming the poor habits by learning good ones.

According to Bernard P. McCabe, Jr., in *Communicative Voice and Articulation*: "Articulation is the way to clarity in speaking. The key to articulation is accurate production and correct use of consonants. . . .

"Without consonants speech would probably resemble a howl with meaning dependent upon variations in quality of sound. Fortunately, such a situation need not exist. With the consonant there is articulation and speech becomes more efficient" (p. 79).

In other words, speech will not be clear unless the sounds called consonants are articulated properly. The consonants are generally arranged into four groups:

Plosive—as the *p* in "poise," the *b* in "boss," the *t* in "tame," the *d* in "dance," the *g* in "game," the *c* in "cat"

Glide—as the *wh* in "white," the *w* in "wonder," the *r* in "road," the *y* in "you," the *l* in "lip," the *ch* in "check," the *j* in "just"

Fricative—as the *f* in "fun," the *s* in "sip," the *v* in "vain," the *z* in "zippy," the *th* in "think," the *th* in "this," the *sh* in "should," the *s* in "vision,"

Nasal—as the *m* in "make," the *n* in "noise," the *ng* in "youngster," the *h* in "how."

Improper articulation of any of these sounds will make one's speech difficult to understand. How articulate are you in producing the sounds of speech—the sounds of the consonants?

There are many faults in articulation, but three of the most common have to do with:

1. The final *t*, as in "went." The *t* is made silent (not articulated) and the result sounds like "wen"—or as in can't the word becomes "can" (which could be a costly error).

2. The final *ng*, as in "going." The *ng* sound becomes silent, and the word becomes "goin'"—or as in "thinking" the word becomes "thinkin'."

3. The initial *th* in "them" becomes a *d* and the word becomes "dem"—or, in the case of "those," it becomes "dose."

Breaking a bad habit is never easy; it takes patience and work. This applies to breaking poor speech habits. A good book, such as McCabe's, contains many suggestions and exercises by which poor articulation can be corrected. If you do not speak clearly because of poor articulation, you can overcome the defect. Record your speech and then listen to yourself. If you don't like what you hear, do something about it. Practice until you speak clearly and distinctly.

Take care that in attempting to correct the defects you don't go to the extreme and articulate overprecisely. It is annoying and sometimes humorous to listen to someone who overarticulates the *t*'s and the *d*'s and the *p*'s.

Remember the counsel in *Gospel Workers*: "Ministers and teachers should discipline themselves to articulate clearly and distinctly, allowing the full sound to every word" (p. 91). The same applies to anyone who serves as preacher and spokesperson for God.

Proper breathing, pitch, and articulation—these three factors are to be considered when striving for clarity in preaching. Will what you say be clearly understood the next time you speak?

7

The Preacher

Why would anyone want to be a preacher? The task seems almost thankless, and it has never been free of criticism. Paul writes of those who criticized him: "For they say, 'His letters are weighty and strong, but his bodily presence is weak, and his speech of no account'" (2 Cor. 10:10). Or hear him when he writes to Timothy: "For the time is coming when people will not endure sound teaching, but having itching ears they will accumulate for themselves teachers to suit their own likings, and will turn away from listening to the truth and wander into myths" (2 Tim. 4:3, 4).

As Clyde Fant points out in *Preaching for Today* (pages 5-7), the literature on preaching in every age is filled with criticisms, calls for renewal, dire predictions, and alarms with respect to the present and future state of the preaching art. To illustrate the point, Fant lists a number of titles of articles written in the nineteenth and twentieth centuries: "Defects of Preaching," 1805; "Bad Preaching," 1868; "Dull Sermons," 1876; "Is the Modern Pulpit a Failure?" 1878; "Is the Power of the Pulpit Waning?" 1899; "The Decadence of Preaching," 1903; "Why Sermons Make Us Go to Sleep," 1908; "Is Preaching Obsolete?" 1911; "Is Preaching Futile?" 1920; "Can the Protestant Sermon Survive?" 1932.

Actually, Fant's book is only one of a number published in

the past 10 years that start by commenting on the crisis of the pulpit, such as Thor Hall's *The Future Shape of Preaching* and Colin Morris's *The Word and the Words*. Chester Pennington's *God Has a Communication Problem* begins with these words: "Almost everybody in the churches today—lay and clergy alike—agree that preaching is in trouble and indeed has been for some time" (p. 1).

It would seem to be one of the miracles of all time that preaching has survived and continues to this day. But it has survived, because preaching partakes of the very essence and soul of Christianity. There can be no authentic Christianity without preaching.

The Preacher as Witness

Hear the words of Jesus—the last words to His disciples before His return to heaven: "And you shall be my witnesses in Jerusalem and in all Judea and Samaria and to the end of the earth" (Acts 1:8). *You shall be My witnesses.* And that is what they became. Wherever they went they witnessed.

They witnessed by what they did. They healed the sick, ministered to the poor, cast out devils, lived the holy life. But they also did a lot of talking. As witnesses, they gave their testimony. They testified in proclaiming the truth as it is in Jesus, the truth about God—who He is, what He is like, His purpose and will for the world, and how He intends that His purposes shall be fulfilled. But more than that, they testified in sharing an experience.

They shared their experience because it was indispensable to their testimony. They had lived with Jesus. They were there that day when He lost many of His followers. His "sayings" had become unacceptable. Some said, "This is a hard saying; who can listen to it?" And so, according to John's Gospel, chapter 6, verse 66: "After this many of his disciples drew back and no longer went with him." But what interests us is what followed. Seeing so many leave, Jesus turned to the twelve and said, "Do you also wish to go away?" To which Peter replied, "Lord, to whom shall we go? You have the words of eternal life; and we have believed, and have come to know, that you are the Holy One of God" (verses 67-69).

But now Jesus had left them, and the last words they heard Him say were "You shall be my witnesses." What would you expect them to do? Witness. With the kind of conviction that burned within their hearts, how could they do otherwise? Peter stood up in court and said:

"Rulers of the people and elders, if we are being examined today concerning a good deed done to a cripple, by what means this man has been healed, be it known to you all, and to all the people of Israel, that by the name of Jesus Christ of Nazareth, whom you crucified, whom God raised from the dead, by him this man is standing before you well. This is the stone which was rejected by you builders, but which has become the head of the corner. And there is salvation in no one else, for there is no other name under heaven given among men by which we must be saved" (Acts 4:8-12). And both Peter and John continued: "Whether it is right in the sight of God to listen to you rather than to God, you must judge; *for we cannot but speak of what we have seen and heard*" (verses 19, 20).

"We must obey God rather than men. The God of our fathers raised Jesus whom you killed by hanging him on a tree. God exalted him at his right hand as Leader and Savior, to give repentance to Israel and forgiveness of sins. *And we are witnesses to these things*, and so is the Holy Spirit whom God has given to those who obey him" (Acts 5:29-32).

Peter proclaimed the truth: "By the name of Jesus Christ of Nazareth, whom you crucified, whom God raised from the dead, by him this man is standing before you well. . . . There is salvation in no one else, for there is no other name under heaven given among men by which we must be saved." He and John also shared an experience: "we cannot but speak of what we have seen and heard." And he and the apostles said that "we are witnesses to these things."

Paul, in writing to the believers in Corinth, says: "Now I would remind you, brethren, in what terms I preached to you the gospel. . . . For I delivered to you as of first importance what I also received, that Christ died for our sins in accordance with the scriptures, that he was buried, that he was raised on the third day in accordance with the scriptures. . . . Last of all, as to one untimely born, he appeared also to me. For I am the least of the apostles, unfit to be called an apostle, because I persecuted the church of God. But by the grace of God I am what I am, and his grace toward me was not in vain" (1 Cor. 15:1-10).

He proclaimed the truth: "Christ died for our sins in accordance with the scriptures, . . . he was buried, . . . he was raised on the third day." He shared an experience: "I am the least of the apostles, . . . because I persecuted the church of God. But by the grace of God I am what I am, and his grace toward me was not in vain."

Writing to the church, John says: "That which was from the beginning, which we have heard, which we have seen with our eyes, which we have looked upon and touched with our hands, concerning the word of life—the life was made manifest, and we saw it, and testify to it, and proclaim to you the eternal life which was with the Father and was made manifest to us—that which we have seen and heard we proclaim also to you, so that you may have fellowship with us; and our fellowship is with the Father and with his Son Jesus Christ" (1 John 1:1-3).

John shared an experience: "We have heard, . . . we have seen with our eyes, . . . we have . . . touched with our hands." He proclaimed the truth: "The life was made manifest, . . . the eternal life which was with the Father and was manifest to us . . . ; and our fellowship is with the Father and with his Son Jesus Christ."

From the testimony of Paul noted above (1 Cor. 15), it would seem that there was a concern on the part of the apostles in witnessing to interpret Jesus, His life and ministry, according to the Scriptures. In this they were following the example of Christ Himself, who, "beginning with Moses and all the prophets, . . . interpreted to them in all the scriptures the things concerning himself" (Luke 24:27). It would be natural, then, for the early Christians when meeting together to use the Scriptures in witnessing in order to understand

Christ better. Coming from Judaism, they were accustomed to having the Scriptures interpreted as a part of the synagogue service. It is not surprising, then, that one of the earliest records we have of a postbiblical Christian meeting described by Justin Martyr in his *Dialogue With Trypho the Jew* tells of a service in which someone reads from the writings of the apostles or prophets and the president instructs or exhorts "to the imitation of these good things." This was later to be called the sermon—the exposition of the Word at the time of worship.

Preaching is witnessing, a continuation of what the first Christians did by virtue of the fact that they were Christians, disciples of Christ. Wherever they went, they talked about Christ. They proclaimed Him to the unbeliever and they exhorted one another concerning Him when they met together. They proclaimed the truth and they shared an experience.

When you proclaim the truth, do you share an experience?

There are times when you do this explicitly—you share what Christ means or has meant to you. At other times it should be done implicitly.

An actor was asked to repeat the twenty-third psalm. He did so with great effectiveness. His diction and articulation was flawless; his tone, mellifluous; his inflection and tempo, expressive. At the close he received a standing ovation.

When all was quiet again, having spotted a preacher in the audience, the actor called him to the stage and asked him if he would repeat the same psalm. The preacher consented, and at the close of his presentation there was complete silence. The audience was rapt in thoughtful contemplation, and many an eye was filled with tears.

Standing beside the preacher, the actor put his arm around him and addressed the audience: "Ladies and gentlemen, we both repeated the same psalm, but obviously there was a difference, and the difference is this: I know the psalm, but this man knows the Shepherd."

When you preach, the congregation should know that

you know the Shepherd. Preaching is not only a proclamation of the truth—it is also the sharing of an experience. As a preacher you are more than a speechmaker—you are a witness. Which is to say that your effectiveness as a preacher depends as much upon *how* your hearers perceive you as a person as it does on *what* you say and how you say it. Do they see you as a person of good Christian character, fully committed to Christ, one who is loving and compassionate while at the same time just and firm in support of the right? This is why a person who is not a gifted orator can be a successful preacher.

If your congregation loves and trusts you, what you say may not be delivered in golden tones, and it may not be overpoweringly brilliant, but it speaks to the heart and convicts the soul. This is not to say that all the principles of good communication may be ignored as long as one is a noble Christian. If that were so, the preparation of this guide to preaching would be for naught. What it does say is that one cannot be an effective preacher by wits alone.

In classical rhetoric, the way the speaker impresses the audience was called "ethos." It is also called "personal proof" or "source credibility." In verifying the facts, we often consider the source. We also say "Actions speak louder than words."

The Unspoken Word

What does a preacher who comes shuffling onto the platform all slouched over, arms flapping awkwardly, the embodiment of discoordination, "say" to you? If for some reason he or she is afflicted with crippling physical defects, that is one thing. But if the awkwardness is because of a lack of concern for proper appearance in public, that is another matter altogether.

Remember, your appearance on the platform speaks to your congregation even before you stand at the pulpit. According to Albert Mehrabian, as cited by Haddon Robinson in *Biblical Preaching*, "only 7 percent of the impact of a speaker's message comes through his words; 38 percent springs from his voice, 55 percent from facial expressions" (p. 193).

Pulpit posture is important. For the most part you should stand and walk erect. The spinal column is not a crutch, but a backbone. The pulpit is not a pedestal upon which to drape your body. It is sometimes called an altar, but it is not intended that your physical person be sacrificed thereon. The pulpit is for the purpose of holding your Bible and notes and your hands in restful repose from time to time. And don't give the congregation the impression that if the pulpit were taken away you would collapse in a heap on the floor. An occasional leaning over the pulpit as a gesture is one thing; using it for a prop is another.

Do you slouch in your chair on the platform to the point where the audience has a hard time seeing your face for your knees? That is an overstatement, to be sure, but perhaps the point needs special emphasis. Don't be so stiff that people are uncomfortable looking at you. Sit in the chair relaxed but alive, interested in what is happening, aware of the fact that you are, after all, in the house of God. To sleep is, of course, a no-no. But to close your eyes and give the impression that you are asleep accomplishes the same thing as far as the audience is concerned. If you are not interested in what is happening, why should they be?

And then there is the matter of dress and grooming. Social standards with respect to hairstyles and clothing are much more liberal today than in previous years, but the people you speak to are still sensitive to what you look like. A person who is essentially self-centered may say, "It's nobody's business what I wear or how I look," but you who seek to communicate the gospel may very well defeat your purposes by such independence. In this respect you will need to ask certain questions. What is appropriate to the place and the occasion? There is a difference between the church and the campground or the nature trail. There is a difference between the Sabbath day and the other days of the week. We would do well to heed the counsel of Ellen G. White on this point: "Many need instruction as to how they should appear in the assembly for worship on the Sabbath. They are not to enter the presence of God in the common clothing worn during the week. All should have a special Sabbath suit, to be worn when attending service in God's house" (*Testimonies*, vol. 6, p. 355).

"Especial care will be taken to dress in a manner that will show a sacred regard for the holy Sabbath and the worship of God" (*Messages to Young People*, p. 349).

What is appropriate to the congregation? There is a difference between the young and the old—and it is not always just a matter of age. But do not invite one group to question your character in an endeavor to appeal to the other. It may not seem fair that either group should judge your integrity and sincerity by the way you comb your hair, but when such is the case, you gain nothing by ignoring the fact. While on the one hand you do not want to offend your audience by your appearance, you cannot always, and often must not, identify with your congregation to win their acceptance. For instance, you need not look like a tramp to win a tramp. In fact, the tramp would probably laugh at your naivete. Instead of winning his approval or confidence, you would probably impress him as being phony and devious, which might not be too far from the truth. The key word here is "appropriate." You want to identify with the congregants and win their confidence, but you cannot afford to be dishonest and without principle. You cannot sacrifice modesty for the sake of expediency.

Something that, in most instances, will greatly trouble you as a novice or nonprofessional preacher is the question of gestures or body language. Should you move from behind the pulpit or walk back and forth across the platform? Should you make gestures with your hands and arms, and should they be frequent or seldom, sweeping or reserved? It depends a great deal upon your personality.

If you have an image of the preacher as one who is dynamic and even bombastic in these respects, the tendency will be for you to function in keeping with that image. But that image may not fit your personality and the results may be awkward, distracting, and embarrassing. Since it is not natural for you to function this way, you will feel self-conscious and uncomfortable, and your congregation will feel embarrassment for you. Your preaching will be affected.

My counsel to young preachers is *"Let* it happen, don't *make* it happen. Be yourself." If you feel the moods in your sermon in keeping with what you are saying, the gestures will follow and be natural. All of us speak with some body language. The language of a naturally bombastic person will be that way, whereas the language of a more subdued person will be more subdued. Some speak effectively with slight gestures, mainly movements of the head. It is surprising how a slight movement of the head can be effective as a gesture, but it must be natural. Mercy to the person who prompts himself or herself with signals in the margin of the notes as to what gestures to use here and which to use there!

Keep in mind that a gesture is for the purpose of drawing a picture. If the gesture is to portray a long journey, it will, by the very nature of things, be relatively long and sweeping. If it is to indicate the location of heaven, it will point upward (certainly not downward). If it is to describe a circle, it may call for the use of one hand or both hands, depending somewhat on the size of the circle. If it is to represent speeding or running swiftly, it will move swiftly. Again, the key is to let it happen.

The image of the bombastic, fire-and-brimstone preacher is somewhat classic and the object of considerable humor. In a little church in Scotland the pulpit was mounted high on the front wall and entered through a door at floor level and up a short flight of stairs behind the wall. The church could not afford a full-time pastor, so visiting preachers came from time to time to provide the sermon. The sexton was a large burly man who always led the preacher down the aisle, ushering him to the door of the pulpit. On this particular Sunday the preacher was rather small in stature and provided somewhat of a spectacle as he followed the big sexton down the aisle. Upon arriving at the door to the pulpit, the sexton unlocked the door, which was his custom, letting the preacher pass through, and then locked the door again and sat in a nearby pew with arms folded across his chest.

The little preacher, having mounted the steps, entered the pulpit with head and shoulders barely visible. But what he lacked in size he made up for in sound and fury. From time to time he would hit the pulpit with his fist in order to drive the point home, and perhaps with the intent of waking the sleeping saints.

In the congregation was a little girl sitting beside her father. When the preaching began, she was a bit frightened by the noise and reached for her father's hand for comfort and security. Before long she was sitting in her father's lap and hanging on to his coat for dear life. Suddenly, in drawing his sermon to a close, the preacher hit the pulpit with his fist, creating a clap of thunder that echoed throughout the church. Then he paused for effect, and in the quiet of that pause the worshipers heard the little girl say, as she gazed wide-eyed into her father's face, "Father, if he could get out of there, he'd kill the lot of us, wouldn't he?"

Be careful. You have not been called to the business of scaring little girls or of killing congregations.

There is no rule governing whether or not you should leave the pulpit to stand beside it for the purpose of getting closer to the hearers and speaking to them more directly. This will depend upon how you feel about it. Don't do it just because you think you should. The tendency today in the media is to speak without a lectern or pulpit. You seldom see a person on television speaking from behind one. This has prompted some preachers to all but dispense with the pulpit. I have no quarrel with that. In fact, at times, when a number of empty pews have separated me from the congregation, I have left the pulpit entirely and stood in the aisle so I could be closer to my congregation. It is important for me to generate a dynamic flow and interchange between me and my listeners. Not that audible dialogue is taking place, but hopefully we are communicating psychologically.

The main problem in walking back and forth from one side of the pulpit to another is that it becomes distracting if you have reached that point when you give the impression that you are a caged wild animal behind bars, consumed by a madness to be set free. People do not generally enjoy listening to a sermon and following the movements of the preacher as if they were watching a tennis match.

As a general rule, start your sermon while standing behind the pulpit (if there is one). Let the center of gravity run through the balls of your feet. In this position you are prepared to move in whatever way seems best. If the center of gravity runs through your heels, you will feel off balance the minute you move. From the proper, balanced position, let the Spirit move you. If you feel the sermon as it develops, the movements should come naturally.

Another common problem for novice preachers is that of nervous body movement, especially of the hands. One hand will pump away as if giving special emphasis to everything that is said. The gesture signifies nothing except that the speaker is nervous. This can happen without the speaker even being aware of it. Blessed is the preacher who has a spouse or good friend who will point out this or any other distractions that creep into delivery. If you are having trouble with nervous hand movements, try preaching with your hands behind you. You will not want to do this for the whole sermon, but as often as you do, it will eliminate the distraction for your hearers. You can move hands and fingers a great deal when your hands are behind you, and no one facing you will know the difference. Those sitting behind you on the platform may be distracted, but better that a few should suffer than the whole congregation perish! Try speaking with your arms and hands beside you hanging comfortably from your shoulders. With a little practice, this can be very comfortable. From this position you can gesture as you feel you should. We call this the home position. It is the position you return to when not gesturing. Another home position is letting the hands rest on either side of the pulpit. This is natural and comfortable. Gripping the pulpit as if it were going to leave you is uncomfortable and obvious to the audience.

The key to good preaching, especially in the area of body language, is relaxation. It is nervousness that makes your hands pump, your body wiggle, etc. You move to expend nervous energy. Overcoming nervousness is not easy. We are all afraid of standing before an audience and performing in any way. But we can learn how to handle it with experience. As with any other skill, the more it is done, the more comfortable it becomes.

One of the keys to relaxation is deep breathing. The more oxygen in the system, the more comfortable you will be. Nervousness mounts as the body is starved for oxygen. Notice how short of breath you are when you get nervous. That is because you are not breathing deeply enough. Often, just before going to the pulpit, I will take several deep breaths. This is because I am most nervous at the beginning of the sermon. Once into the sermon, I tend to relax and everything becomes much easier and more enjoyable.

One of the reasons you are nervous when speaking before a congregation is the fear of not remembering what you have to say. The irony of it all is that the harder you try to remember, the more nervous you become and the easier it is to forget. Mental block is a state that affects us all at some time or other. At this point it might help to recall or reread what I said earlier about preaching with good eye contact and freedom from notes. As suggested, fix in mind those elements of the sermon that are critical so that you can remember them though the heavens fall. Trying to remember the whole sermon word for word only complicates the situation. In preaching, we must always keep in mind that we are not on our own. We pray for the guidance of the Holy Spirit and trust that, when we have prepared well, He will bring to mind that which He has helped us prepare and that which He would have us say. Dependence upon the Spirit bears repeating as we consider the work of preaching. We will be largely ineffective without His power and presence.

In matters of "source credibility" and "visible code" these words are worth noting: "The minister must remember that favorable or unfavorable impressions are made upon his hearers by his deportment in the pulpit, his attitude, his manner of speaking, his dress. He should cultivate courtesy and refinement of manner, and should carry himself with a quiet dignity becoming to his high calling. Solemnity and a certain godly authority mingled with meekness should characterize his demeanor. Coarseness and rudeness are not to be tolerated in the common walks of life, much less should they be permitted in the work of the ministry. The minister's attitude should be in harmony with the holy truths he proclaims. His word should be in every respect earnest and well chosen. . . .

"God expects His ministers, in their manners and in their dress, to give a fitting representation of the principles of truth and the sacredness of their office. They are to set an example that will help men and women to reach a high standard" (*Gospel Workers*, pp. 172-174).

Remember that the one who wrote, "I have become all things to all men, that I might by all means save some" (1 Cor. 9:22), also wrote, "Whether you eat or drink, or *whatever you do*, do all to the glory of God" (1 Cor. 10:31).

8

Give It Your Best

Preparing a good sermon takes time. It is a creative enterprise and therefore challenges a person's inner resources, because what is created is born of the soul. But as a lay leader, the time you give to the work of the church is limited. You are not a professional public speaker or preacher. Therefore, you may have to settle for less than the ideal. But you are not excused from doing your very best. You are not free to step into the pulpit on Sabbath morning and just fill the hour. The pulpit is not the place for you to tell of your trips abroad, the churches you have visited, and the wonderful Adventist friends you have met, except as you use such experiences to illustrate a point. The pulpit is not the place for you to ride some hobbyhorse of doctrine (no matter how basic it may be), to whip the saints for being so unsaintly, or to fumble and stumble through some article you have read.

Many stories can and have been told of things heard from the pulpit that would be humorous if they were not so tragic! But all this need not be. Some of the principles and procedures outlined in this book will help get the task done properly and in less time than it would take to do it in a haphazard way. It may not seem that way at first. But as the principles are applied and experience is gained, the task will seem far less burdensome.

You may have read an article that you would like to share with your brothers and sisters on Sabbath morning. You may have come across something that is inspiring and helpful. You may feel impressed by the Holy Spirit that this is what you ought to bring to the church the next time you are called upon to preach. Very well. But do so without presenting it in a boring manner, without reading it word for word, void of expression and life.

Using a good article from the *Adventist Review* or *Signs of the Times* or a chapter from a book (written perhaps by Ellen G. White) or a published sermon (or one you have heard) does save time and effort. But the key to using such material is to make it your own! Caution should be used, of course, so as to avoid plagiarism—credit should be given where credit is due, but you can make it your own without claiming credit for it in a dishonest way. What I mean is this: Analyze the article or the body of material. What is the central theme? How is the theme amplified? What are the major divisions, the subdivisions? Make an outline, see how it all fits together. As you do this you may see where you can add a thought of your own here and there, where you can insert an illustration of your own. After you have taken the time to study it in this way, it will become more a part of you. You will fix the main thought and supporting ideas in your mind, and you can then verbalize it all in your own style. When the message has gotten into you, you can share it as yours and do so with conviction and enthusiasm.

A sermon like this may well begin with the words "This morning I would like to share with you something I read in . . ." (or "something I heard . . ."). At times during the presentation it might be well to read word for word what the author wrote, because to use his or her exact words might make the point more effective. But for the most part it should be *your* presentation, *your* delivery, *your* style, *your* witness to the truth of what is said. Few things are more deadly than a sermon that sounds canned. Take it out of the can, give it life, give it shoes, make it walk!

Be jealous for the flock entrusted to your care. Guard the pulpit and the sermon hour so that the Word of God may be heard in His house. You have been given a high calling. Honor that calling with sacrifice and dedication. Give yourself to the preaching of the Word, and it will amaze you what God can do through you—even *you* who wish you had an Aaron to do your speaking for you!

In this book no attempt has been made to cover all the aspects of homiletical theory. The emphasis has been upon basics for the novice and nonprofessional preacher. For those interested in further and continued study on the subject of preaching, there is a whole library available, and more books on the subject are being printed every year. In addition to those already mentioned in the chapters above, the bibliography includes a few others that I have found most helpful. "Now to him who is able to strengthen you according to my gospel and the preaching of Jesus Christ, according to the revelation of the mystery which was kept secret for long ages, but is now disclosed and through the prophetic writings is made known to all nations, according to the command of the eternal God, to bring about the obedience of faith—to the only wise God be glory for evermore through Jesus Christ! Amen" (Rom. 16:25-27).

Bibliography

Adams, Jay E. *Pulpit Speech*. Grand Rapids: Baker Book House, 1971.

Anderson, Virgil A. *Training the Speaking Voice*. New York: Oxford University Press, 1961.

Barclay, William. *The Daily Study Bible Series*. Revised Edition. Philadelphia: The Westminster Press, 1975.

Black, John W., and Ruth B. Erwin. *Voice and Diction*. Columbus, Ohio: Charles E. Merrill Co., 1969.

Bradford, Charles E. *Preaching to the Times*. Washington, D.C.: Review and Herald Pub. Ass., 1975.

Broadus, John A. *On the Preparation and Delivery of Sermons*. New York: Harper and Brothers, 1944.

Cox, James W. *Preaching*. San Francisco: Harper and Row, 1985.

Craddock, Fred B. *Preaching*. Nashville: Abingdon Press, 1985.

Crum, Milton, Jr. *Manual on Preaching*. Valley Forge, Pa: Judson Press, 1977.

Evans, I. H. *The Preacher and His Preaching*. Washington, D.C.: Review and Herald Pub. Assn., 1938.

Fant, Clyde E. *Preaching for Today*. San Francisco: Harper and Row, 1975.

Hall, Thor. *The Future Shape of Preaching*. Philadelphia:

Fortress Press, 1971.

Haynes, Carlyle B. *The Divine Art of Preaching*. Washington, D. C.: Review and Herald Pub. Assn., 1939.

Hoefler, Richard Carl. *Creative Preaching and Oral Writing*. Lima, Ohio: C.S.S. Publishing Co., 1978.

Holmes, C. Raymond. *The Last Word*. Berrien Springs, Mich.: Andrews University Press, 1987.

Horne, Chevis F. *Crisis in the Pulpit*. Grand Rapids, Mich.: Baker Book House, 1975.

Hybels, Bill, Stuart Briscoe, and Haddon Robinson. *Mastering Contemporary Preaching*. Portland, Ore.: Multnomah, 1989.

The Interpreter's Bible. New York: Abingdon Press. Vols. 1-12.

Johnson, Herrick. *The Ideal Ministry*. New York: Fleming H. Revell Co., 1908.

Koller, Charles W. *Expository Preaching Without Notes*. Grand Rapids: Baker Book House, 1962.

Lenski, R.C.H. *The Sermon, Its Homiletical Construction*. Grand Rapids: Baker Book House, 1969.

Lewis, Ralph L., and Gregg Lewis. *Inductive Preaching*. Westchester, Ill.: Crossway Books, 1983.

Lowry, Eugene L. *The Homiletical Plot*. Atlanta: John Knox Press, 1980.

Luccock, Halford E. *In the Minister's Workshop*. New York: Abingdon-Cokesbury Press, 1944.

McCabe, Bernard P., Jr. *Communicative Voice and Articulation*. Boston: Holbrook Press, 1970.

Macpherson, Ian. *The Art of Illustrating Sermons*. New York: Abingdon Press, 1964.

Monroe, Alan H. *Principles and Types of Speech*, revised edition. Chicago: Scott Foresman, 1939.

Morris, Colin. *The Word and the Words*. New York: Abingdon Press, 1975.

Mounce, Robert H. *The Essential Nature of New Testament Preaching*. Grand Rapids: William B. Eerdmans Pub. Co., 1960.

Pennington, Chester. *God Has a Communication Problem*.

New York: Hawthorn Books, Inc., 1976.

Perry, Lloyd M. *Biblical Preaching for Today's World*. Chicago: Moody Press, 1973.

Pitt-Watson, Ian. *A Primer for Preachers*. Grand Rapids: Baker Book House, 1986.

Reu, M. *Homiletics: A Manual of the Theory and Practice of Preaching*. Grand Rapids: Baker Book House, 1967.

Richards, H.M.S. *Feed My Sheep*. Washington, D.C.: Review and Herald Pub. Assn., 1958.

Robinson, Haddon W. *Biblical Preaching*. Grand Rapids: Baker Book House, 1980.

Sangster, William E. *The Craft of Sermon Construction*. Philadelphia: Westminster Press, 1950.

_____. *The Craft of Sermon Illustration*. Philadelphia: Westminster Press, 1957.

The Seventh-day Adventist Bible Commentary, Vols. 1-7. Washington, D.C.: Review and Herald Pub. Assn.

Seventh-day Adventist Bible Dictionary. Washington, D.C.: Review and Herald Pub. Assn., 1960.

Unger, Merrill F. *Principles of Expository Preaching*. Grand Rapids: Zondervan Publishing House, 1955.

Van Dolson, Leo R. *Hidden No Longer*. Mountain View, Calif.: Pacific Press Pub. Assn., 1968.

Vos, Howard. *Effective Bible Study*. Grand Rapids: Zondervan Pub. House, 1956.

White, Ellen G. *The Acts of the Apostles*. Mountain View, Calif.: Pacific Press Pub. Assn., 1911.

_____. *The Desire of Ages*. Mountain View, Calif.: Pacific Press Pub. Assn., 1898.

_____. *Gospel Workers*. Washington, D.C.: Review and Herald Pub. Assn., 1948.

_____. *The Great Controversy*, Mountain View, Calif.: Pacific Press Pub. Assn. 1888-1911.

_____. *Messages to Young People*. Nashville: Southern Pub. Assn., 1930.

_____. *Patriarchs and Prophets*. Mountain View, Calif.: Pacific Press Pub. Assn., 1890, 1913.

BIBLIOGRAPHY

_____. *Prophets and Kings*. Mountain View, Calif.: Pacific Press Pub. Assn., 1917.

_____. *Testimonies for the Church*. Oakland, Calif.: Pacific Press Pub. Assn., 1885-1911.

_____. *Testimonies to Ministers*. Mountain View, Calif.: Pacific Press Pub. Assn., 1923.

Wardlaw, Don M. ed. *Preaching Biblically*. Philadelphia: Westminster Press, 1983.

Whitesell, Faris D., and Lloyd M. Perry. *Variety in Your Preaching*. New York: Fleming H. Revell Co., 1954.

Essential Reference Books

The SDA Bible Commentary

This 10-volume set includes seven volumes of verse-by-verse commentary, plus the *SDA Bible Dictionary, SDA Bible Students' Source Book,* and *SDA Encyclopedia.* Supplementary material includes maps, charts, and illustrations.

Volume 1, Genesis to Deuteronomy, US$35.95, Cdn$44.95
Volume 2, Joshua to 2 Kings, US$35.95, Cdn$44.95
Volume 3, 1 Chronicles to Song of Solomon, US$35.95, Cdn$44.95
Volume 4, Isaiah to Malachi, US$35.95, Cdn$44.95
Volume 5, Matthew to John, US$35.95, Cdn$44.95
Volume 6, Acts to Ephesians, US$35.95, Cdn$44.95
Volume 7, Philippians to Revelation, US$35.95, Cdn$44.95
Volume 7-A, *Ellen G. White Comments*, US$18.95, Cdn$23.70
Volume 8, *SDA Bible Dictionary*, US$35.95, Cdn$44.95
Volume 9, *SDA Bible Students' Source Book*, US$35.95, Cdn$44.95
Volume 10, *SDA Encyclopedia*, US$35.95, Cdn$44.95

Complete commentary set (volume 7-A not included), US$329.50, Cdn$412.50

Bible Plants and Animals, 3 volumes

Harry J. Baerg. Beautiful illustrations by this popular artist and naturalist portray every mammal, plant, bird, and other creature mentioned in the Bible. The commentary is filled with enlightening facts about the behavior of the animals and their interaction with man, and which plants were used for food and how they were prepared. Discover a whole new world of meaning and imagery in the Bible with this series of timeless reference books. 144 pages each volume. Hardcover, US$29.95, Cdn$37.45, set. US$11.95, Cdn$14.95 each.

To order, call **1-800-765-6955** or write to ABC Mailing Service, P.O. Box 1119, Hagerstown, MD 21741. Send check or money order. Enclose applicable sales tax and 15 percent (minimum US$2.50) for postage and handling. Prices and availability subject to change without notice. Add 7 percent GST in Canada.

Invaluable Resources for Preachers

Inspiration, by Alden Thompson

Did every fact and idea in the Bible come straight from God? What about inconsistencies in Scripture? If we read the Bible too closely, could we find something that will destroy our faith? How much freedom do we have to interpret the Bible? In this faith-affirming book, Dr. Alden Thompson shows us how to read the Bible so that God's will shines through puzzling commands and apparent contradictions. Hardcover, 332 pages. US$15.95, Cdn$19.95.

What Is God Like? by Caleb Rosado

In this new look at the parables of the lost sheep, coin, and sons, the author breaks down false images of God, enabling us to become reacquainted with a God of great compassion who is eager for our salvation. Paper, 96 pages. US$6.95, Cdn$8.70.

Rebuke and Challenge, by Norman Young

The author explains 11 of Jesus' well-known parables point by point. These stories will captivate your imagination and awaken new spiritual life within you. Paper, 96 pages. US$6.95, Cdn$8.70.

Chariots of Salvation, by Hans LaRondelle

When we center Christ in our interpretation of Armageddon, we do not find fearsome threats of global war, but a comforting promise of divine deliverance for those who trust Him. Helpful for those conducting Revelation seminars. Paper, 192 pages. US$9.95, Cdn$12.45.

To order, call **1-800-765-6955** or write to ABC Mailing Service, P.O. Box 1119, Hagerstown, MD 21741. Send check of money order. Enclose applicable sales tax and 15 percent (minimum US$2.50) for postage and handling. Prices and availability subject to change without notice. Add 7 percent GST in Canada.